NEW ENGLAND FURNITURE AT WILLIAMSBURG

The
Williamsburg Decorative Arts Series

GRAHAM HOOD, *Editor*

✺

The Williamsburg Collection of Antique Furnishings

New England Furniture at Williamsburg

New England FURNITURE at Williamsburg

By

BARRY A. GREENLAW

Published by
THE COLONIAL WILLIAMSBURG FOUNDATION
Williamsburg, Virginia
Distributed by
THE UNIVERSITY PRESS OF VIRGINIA
Charlottesville, Virginia

Library of Congress Catalog Card Number 73-90536

Colonial Williamsburg ISBN: paper, 0-87935-019-9; cloth, 0-87935-020-2
University Press of Virginia ISBN: paper, 0-8139-0559-1; cloth, 0-8139-0549-4

PRINTED IN THE UNITED STATES OF AMERICA

Contents

Foreword   vii

Introduction   1

Short-title list   8

The Catalog   9

Index   189

Foreword

FOR ALMOST FIFTY YEARS, with the aid of generous donors, Colonial Williamsburg has been collecting appropriate objects for exhibition in the Historic Area of the restored Virginia capital. These furnishings blend with the other major appeals of Williamsburg—its handcrafts, gardens and greens, colonial architecture, preservation research, and interpretation of the heritage of eighteenth-century Virginia—to make a visit to Williamsburg a true rendezvous with the nation's past.

Though the Williamsburg collection has long been recognized as one of the world's great assemblages of American and English antiques, its 100,000 or more objects have been only briefly, and partially, known by those who have visited our exhibition buildings.

This scholarly catalog of one category of our important holdings is the first of a series that will eventually embrace the entire collection. It is fitting that this opening volume should deal with New England furniture, since the first piece accessioned in 1930 was a small serpentine-front card table (No. 140 in this catalog), a New England object with a history of Virginia ownership.

The great diversity of the collection revealed here is a reflection of the policy established by Mr. John D. Rockefeller, Jr., who felt that every object acquired should aid in the interpretation of life in eighteenth-century Williamsburg. From the start he insisted on appropriateness as well as authenticity. For that reason—since they are designed to help interpret the social history of an era—we have acquired objects ranging from fine portraits to harness for horses, from elegant bookcases to iron kitchen implements, from silver snuffboxes to the crude tools of shinglemakers. Together, on display in the more than two hundred rooms of our exhibition buildings, these objects picture the broad range of a society that included royal governors and men of vast wealth as well as artisans, manual laborers, indentured servants, and slaves. In combination with documentary evidence and excavated artifacts, our collections offer an imposing record of eighteenth-century Virginia.

The collections have been assembled over the years by resourceful curators who built upon the foundation laid by the early consultants, William Graves Perry, Mrs. Susan Higginson Nash, and Louis Guerineau Myers. From Mr. Myers, then treasurer of the Rockefeller Foundation and a highly respected collector, the restoration acquired several important examples of New England furniture. Several of these pieces, first exhibited in New York in the famous Girl Scout Loan Show of 1929, are included in this volume.

James L. Cogar, who served as our first official curator (1931–50), made invaluable contributions and acquired many notable pieces. One important object listed in this volume, an acquisition of 1935, is a superb bombé chest-on-chest (No. 81) acquired from the estate of the well-known collector, Francis G. Shaw.

Mr. Cogar's successor, John M. Graham II, devoted twenty years to expanding the scope and improving the quality of the collection. Appropriately enough, his first purchase was the unique low-post bed with carved busts on the foot posts (No. 3). It is one of the more important objects listed in this book, and, indeed, in the entire Colonial Williamsburg collection.

Succeeding collectors, including Graham Hood, the present curator, have added many important objects; one quarter of the items cataloged here have been acquired since 1970.

We are grateful to the Ford Foundation, which made possible this publication under its program for Catalogs of Fine Arts Collections, and this is one of three catalogs in our series to be sponsored by the Ford Foundation.

Companion catalogs of the collection will soon be published as part of our continuing effort to provide information to our visitors and friends. In addition, we are preparing abstracts of the catalogs, in the form of small booklets, to be sold at modest prices. In this way we hope to share the fruits of long and painstaking research with the widest possible audience as well as to interest prospective donors in sharing our quest to improve both the quality and scope of the Colonial Williamsburg collections.

—Carlisle H. Humelsine
President
The Colonial Williamsburg Foundation

Introduction

The people of New England being obliged to apply themselves to manufactures more than other of the plantations, who have the benefit of a better soil, the warmer climate, such improvements have been lately made there in all sorts of mechanic arts, that not only escritoires, chairs, and other wooden manufactures, but hoes, axes and other iron utensils, are now exported from thence to the other plantations.[1]

THE FACT THAT FURNITURE made in New England was exported to the southern colonies in the eighteenth century is not a recent discovery. During the early decades of the twentieth century when many of the pioneer collectors of American furniture were establishing their collections, the South was an important source of supply. Boatloads of furniture, much of it of New England origin, made the reverse trip northward, its previous history lost forever. One of the best descriptions of one of these "raids" is a fictitious but thinly disguised tale of a trip by three northern collectors to "Richwood" and "Petersville," Virginia, in the 1920s "where two thirds of the poultry in the suburban districts have reared their broods for more than half a century in rare old Heppelwhite sideboards, magnificent old cabriole-legged scrutoires, or exquisite old block-front chests-on-chests that the old families of old Virginia long ago relegated to the old barn...."[2]

In a more scholarly vein, *Antiques* published a short pioneer study of the coastal trade in furniture in 1932,[3] a more thorough article was written by Mabel Munson Swan in the same magazine in 1949,[4] and a specialized study by Henry W. Belknap on the significant Salem trade of the early nineteenth century appeared in 1949 in the Essex Institute Historical Collections.[5]

Only recently, however, has a substantial effort been made to determine the extent of the eighteenth-century coastal trade in furniture from New England to the South. Through the fortunate survival of a number of im-

1

portant official documents of the period, it is now possible to determine in part the significance of this trade, at least in Virginia.

The most important of these documents are the Virginia naval officers' reports to the Board of Trade. Beginning in 1720, each of the six naval districts in the colony was required to submit reports (usually quarterly) to the board. The purpose was to prevent fraud in customs and illegal shipping into the colony. The naval officer for each district listed every vessel entering his port, its date of entry, where the vessel came from, where it was bound to, and its general cargo. The same information was required for each vessel clearing the port. The Virginia naval districts and their ports of entry were: Lower District of the James River—Hampton; Upper District of the James—Burwell's Ferry near Williamsburg; York River—Yorktown; South Potomack—on the Potomac River; Rappahannock River—Urbanna; and Eastern Shore—Accomack.

The first specific reference to furniture is found in 1729 when "2 scrutoirs" were brought into the Lower District of the James from Boston on the *Mary Glasgow*. Undoubtedly scattered examples of New England furniture were present in the southern colonies before that date, but firm evidence is lacking to support the supposition. The proximity in time of the 1729 reference to the 1734 report of the Board of Trade quoted at the beginning of this introductory section lends credence to the theory that substantial coastal trade in furniture did not begin much before the fourth decade of the eighteenth century.

A study of the existing naval returns for the six Virginia districts between 1729 and the 1760s is extremely instructive, for it confirms a number of previous theories concerning the furniture trade as well as revealing several surprising elements. During the period surveyed, furniture entered Virginia from the ports of Piscataqua (Portsmouth, New Hampshire); Salem, Massachusetts; Boston; Rhode Island; and New London, Connecticut. Of these, Boston was by far the most important; well over half of the furniture imported into Virginia from New England came from there.

While the importance of Boston in the trade is not unexpected (as that city was the largest in the colonies at the time), the fact that the next most frequent shipments came from the Piscataqua area is more surprising. As early as 1730, shipments of furniture arrived from that port, although significant amounts did not come until later and the trade did not reach a peak until the early 1760s.

The first recorded shipment from Rhode Island was registered at the port of Hampton in 1734. On July 22 of that year the Newport-registered *Success* of Rhode Island entered with "1 Case Draws." Again, substantial amounts of furniture do not seem to have been brought in until the 1750s and 1760s, although small, scattered shipments do appear periodically in the earlier years. In most cases, the specific Rhode Island port from which the furniture was shipped is not listed, and it is difficult to determine whether Newport or Providence was the point of departure, although both are occasionally listed independently as well.

Shipments from Salem are scattered and of little importance until the late 1760s, when more frequent cargoes began to be recorded from that port. More substantial and more surprising are the records of shipments from New London, Connecticut—the first evidence this writer has seen of Connecticut furniture imported into the southern colonies before the Revolution. As early as 1736 five desks entered Hampton on board the New London-registered *Hannah,* and five dozen chairs entered the same port on December 16, 1751.

Two types of furniture predominate in the various shipments from New England ports to Virginia—chairs and desks. Of the two, chairs were far more common, accounting for better than three-quarters of the total furniture imports during the period studied. The majority of the chairs came from two ports, Boston and Piscataqua. In general, there is no qualifying description of the chairs with the exception of occasional mention of "leather" chairs in the 1730s (probably similar to No. 40 in this catalog) and a few references to "house" chairs in the 1750s. The latter term was apparently used to eliminate confusion between conventional chairs and riding chairs, which were also imported on occasion.

References to desks are found throughout the period studied beginning with the "2 scrutoirs" from Boston mentioned previously. Shipments were received from all six ports, with the greatest number entering from Boston, although shipments from Rhode Island became increasingly frequent as the period progressed. The reason for the preponderance of desks in the various shipments is unclear at this time, but New England cabinetmakers probably specialized in making them during the period before the Revolution and found a ready market to the south. The 1734 report of the Board of Trade previously quoted at least partially confirms this speculation, as chairs and desks are the only objects of furniture it specifically mentions as being manufactured and exported. Colonial Williamsburg's collection is quite strong in New England desks of the period, representing most of the various types probably included in the shipments.

As puzzling as the large number of desks in the cargoes of the various ships is the absence of substantial numbers of other furniture forms. The "one dozen tables" that entered the York River on the *Sea Nymph* from New England in 1739 is an exception; the great majority of entries included only one or two tables among large numbers of desks and chairs. Likewise, references to chests and chests of drawers are scattered, with one or two the usual number brought in on any one ship. Only one reference to a bed has been found; the *Lucy* from Providence brought in "2 sets of mahogany bed posts" to Yorktown in 1766. Several small shipments of looking glasses were brought in from Boston in the late 1750s and 1760s.

Although the records are not complete for the entire period, and no doubt more furniture was imported than was listed, the amount and type of New England furniture brought into Virginia during the prerevolutionary period are fairly clear. Much less clear, however, is what happened to these imported pieces. Very few records survive to indicate who in Virginia acquired this furniture or how they used it. One notable exception is the inventory of James Jones of King George County, a prosperous carpenter and builder who died in 1744. Included among his possessions were "8 New England flag chairs" and "5 Virginia flag Do." Less specific are the references to "13 Maple chairs" in the 1755 inventory of the estate of John Hamilton of Norfolk County, and "1 Dozen Maple chairs 3.0.0" in the 1770 estate of John Tenham of York County.

Unquestionably the importation of furniture dropped drastically during the revolutionary period, and the surviving records for the period following the war are less precise than before. By the late 1780s, however, enormous shipments of furniture from various New England makers entered southern ports. Well known are the activities of the Sandersons of Salem who, from the late 1780s into the nineteenth century, exported huge quantities of furniture to the South and elsewhere. One ship, the *Ruth*, sailed "to South Carolina and any of the other southern states" with a cargo that included more than 150 pieces of furniture ranging from "Burch" chairs to "Swell'd Mehogany bureaus" to "oak plan bedsteads."[6]

The extent of the trade and the competition from other ports is evidenced by a letter from Captain Elias Grant to Elijah Sanderson, written in Richmond, Virginia, on April 11, 1803:

> ...the goods are not sold as yet part of them are sold. I have tried them twice at vendue but sold very little and what is sold is very lo...the reason they don't sell quick their is Ben a vessel here from New York with furniture & sold it very lo...there is no way of selling goods here but by vendue.[7]

Although records are certainly not complete and additional research is needed, it seems clear that a rather substantial amount of New England furniture found its way into the South during the eighteenth and early nineteenth centuries. Exactly what this furniture was we shall probably never know, but almost certainly much of it paralleled examples in this catalog, particularly the simpler tables, chairs, and desks of which the collection contains so many examples.

The range of objects described and pictured in this catalog spans almost two hundred years of time and varies in quality from the most sophisticated examples of a given form to simple, rather standard items of little artistic merit. Unlike many museums, Colonial Williamsburg has always endeavored to obtain not only the best high-style productions of the major urban centers, but has also made a conscious effort to acquire simple, plain examples of furniture to furnish its several taverns, kitchens, laundries, and the bedrooms of the smaller houses. Thus in this catalog a magnificent block-front piece of Newport furniture may be seen in close proximity to a Windsor chair or a rather crude folding bed. Each of these objects is important in its own way as interpretive material, and to omit the less grand objects from the catalog would fail to convey the whole story.

The New England furniture has been acquired over an almost fifty-year period of time, and it is perhaps inevitable that the collection is weak in certain areas. The most prominent gap is the almost total lack of seventeenth-century examples, although this can be justified to some extent by the absence of documentation for such furniture in the South during the colonial period. Conversely, the collection is particularly strong in such categories as beds (perhaps the finest group in one place in the country), Queen Anne-style chairs, small tables, desks, and Windsor chairs. Outstanding individual pieces include the unique carved bed (No. 3), the superb early block-front clock by William Claggett (No. 83), the famous "Harvard" desk (No. 94), and the graceful Queen Anne marble-top side table (No. 143). The collection also contains a number of signed or otherwise well-documented examples of furniture, several by previously unidentified makers. Altogether, the collection speaks not only of the mechanical dexterity of the mostly anonymous eighteenth-century craftsmen of New England who made the objects, but also of the taste and foresight of the many staff members of Colonial Williamsburg who, over the years, have been responsible for the acquisition and preservation of these pieces.

The catalog is arranged alphabetically by general type and chronologically within each category. Such relatively minor forms as daybeds and sofas are placed under the more inclusive heading "couches." Tables are divided by general type within the larger overall category. Windsor chairs, a specialized form of furniture, are grouped by themselves; this collection is quite rich in them.

Each caption includes all of the basic information known about a given piece. A span of dates is used to indicate the earliest and latest possible date of production. Maximum dimensions of all pieces are given with the exception of chairs, where the width and depth are of the seat. Reference to left and right are to the viewer's left and right. Reference works frequently cited are abbreviated in short title form; complete bibliographical entries for these works may be found following this introduction. The entry "Publ." in the caption is used only to indicate when and where the specific piece under discussion has been previously published.

I am indebted to a great number of people who have made this book possible. Many of the dealers from whom pieces were acquired have willingly provided valuable information and have told me of comparable examples. Nancy Goyne Evans has gladly shared much of her knowledge on the subject of Windsor furniture. Morrison Heckscher was particularly helpful on the subject of easy chairs and Edward LaFond on the clocks. I owe a great deal to John Graham, who first gave me the opportunity to work with the Williamsburg collections; to Milo Naeve, who initially conceived the project of publishing this catalog; to Graham Hood, who read the manuscript, and made many helpful suggestions; and to Carlisle Humelsine, whose vision, foresight, and understanding of the need for catalogs of this sort has been a major factor in its publication. The photographs were taken by Delmore Wenzel, Hans Lorenz, and N. Jane Iseley. Janice Oakes spent innumerable hours researching odd facts, assisting with general details, and typing the entire manuscript several times. Thomas K. Ford edited the manuscript, and Richard Stinely was responsible for the over-all design of the book.

NOTES

1. Report of the Council of Trade and Plantations to the House of Lords, 1734, *Calendar of State Papers, Colonial Series, America and West Indies, 1734–35.* A. P. Newton, ed. (London, 1953), item 20; quoted in *Antiques* 98 (January 1970), p. 58.

2. Kenneth L. Roberts, *Antiquamania* (New York: Doubleday, Doran & Co., Inc., 1928), p. 17.

3. Thomas Hamilton Ormsbee, "Old Tradeways for American Furniture," *Antiques* 22 (September 1932), pp. 109–12.

4. Mabel Munson Swan, "Coastwise Cargoes of Venture Furniture," *Antiques* 55 (April 1949), pp. 278–80.

5. Henry Wyckoff Belknap, "Furniture Exported by Cabinet Makers of Salem," *Essex Institute Historical Collections* 75 (October 1949), pp. 335–57.

6. Swan, op. cit.

7. Mabel Munson Swan, "Elijah and Jacob Sanderson, Early Salem Cabinetmakers" *Essex Institute Historical Collections* 70 (October 1934), p. 333.

SHORT TITLE LIST

CARPENTER

Ralph E. Carpenter, Jr. *The Arts and Crafts of Newport, Rhode Island 1640–1820.* Newport: Preservation Society of Newport County, 1954.

COMSTOCK

Helen Comstock. *American Furniture: Seventeenth, Eighteenth, and Nineteenth Century Styles.* New York: Viking, 1962.

DOWNS

Joseph Downs. *American Furniture in the Henry Francis du Pont Winterthur Museum: Queen Anne and Chippendale Periods.* New York: Macmillan, 1952.

FALES, *Essex County Furniture*

Dean A. Fales, Jr. *Essex County Furniture: Documented Treasures from Local Collections 1660–1860.* Salem, Mass.: Essex Institute, 1965.

FALES, *Painted Furniture*

Dean A. Fales, Jr. *American Painted Furniture 1660–1880.* New York: E. P. Dutton, 1972.

GIRL SCOUTS

Loan Exhibition of Eighteenth and Early Nineteenth Century Furniture and Glass... For the Benefit of the National Council of Girl Scouts, Inc. New York: American Art Galleries, 1929.

HIPKISS

Edwin J. Hipkiss. *Eighteenth Century American Arts; the M. and M. Karolik Collection....* Cambridge: Harvard University Press, 1941.

JOHN BROWN CATALOG

The John Brown House Loan Exhibition of Rhode Island Furniture. Providence: Rhode Island Historical Society, 1965.

KIRK, *Chairs*

John T. Kirk. *American Chairs: Queen Anne and Chippendale.* New York: Alfred A. Knopf, 1972.

KIRK, *Connecticut Furniture*

John T. Kirk. *Connecticut Furniture: Seventeenth and Eighteenth Centuries.* Hartford: Wadsworth Atheneum, 1967.

LOCKWOOD

Luke Vincent Lockwood. *Colonial Furniture in America.* 2 vols. New York: C. Scribner's Sons, 1926.

MONTGOMERY

Charles F. Montgomery. *American Furniture, The Federal Period.* New York: Viking, 1966.

NEW HAMPSHIRE ARTS

The Decorative Arts of New Hampshire, 1725–1825. Manchester, N. H.: Currier Gallery, 1964.

NUTTING, *Pilgrim Century*

Wallace Nutting. *Furniture of the Pilgrim Century.* Framingham, Mass.: Old America Co., 1924.

NUTTING, *Treasury*

Wallace Nutting. *Furniture Treasury.* 3 vols. Framingham, Mass.: Old America Co., 1928–33.

RANDALL

Richard H. Randall, Jr. *American Furniture in the Museum of Fine Arts, Boston.* Boston: Museum of Fine Arts, 1965.

SACK BROCHURES

Opportunities in American Antiques. New York: Israel Sack, Inc., 1956–73.

SACK, *Fine Points*

Albert Sack. *Fine Points of Furniture: Early American.* New York: Crown, 1950.

STONEMAN

Vernon C. Stoneman. *John and Thomas Seymour, Cabinetmakers in Boston, 1794–1816.* Boston: Special Publications, 1959 (Supplement, 1965).

8

THE CATALOG

1

2

1 LOW-POST BED
Massachusetts
1740–70
Maple and white pine

The headboard is white pine; all other elements are maple. Traces of an old red stain can be seen in several areas. (For a discussion of the posts, see below.)

H. 28¾"   L. 74¾"   W. 51"
(73.05 cm.)   (189.89 cm.)   (129.54 cm.)

PROV. Mr. and Mrs. John Halford.

PUBL. William McPherson Hornor, Jr., *Blue Book of Philadelphia Furniture* (Philadelphia: n.p., 1935), pl. 63; *Sack Brochure 5*, No. 244; *Sack Brochure 10*, No. 548; *Antiques* 100 (August 1971), p. 234.

One of the rarest of all forms in American furniture, this bed is the only low-post example known to exist in the fully developed Queen Anne style. Mrs. Nina Fletcher Little owns a New England bed that has probably been cut down from a high octagonal-post example, and Colonial Williamsburg has in its collection a Pennsylvania bed (acc. no. 1954-5) with odd, turned legs terminating in pad feet, more or less influenced by Queen Anne design but probably much later in date.[1] There has always been a question whether this bed also has been cut down from a tall bed. While that is certainly a possibility, the delicacy of the legs seems unsuited to carry additional height and weight, and the manner in which the head posts are finished off seems to preclude the possibility. The profile of the leg, with the pointed knee tapering off sharply to a rounded surface, is characteristic of the North Shore area of Massachusetts. See a similar profile on the small drop-leaf table, No. 132 in this catalog.

1966-225

---

1. *Antiques* 100 (August 1971), p. 234.

2. LOW-POST BED
Newport, Rhode Island
1760–90
Mahogany with birch and white pine

The rails are birch, the headboard is white pine; both have been stained to resemble the mahogany posts. The central talon on the right front foot has been broken off, two talons have been repaired on the left rear leg, and metal braces have been added to the underside of the left side rail at the foot. The headboard is old but probably a replacement—the corners have been shaved off to fit the existing holes in the head posts.

H. 33¼"   L. 77"   W. 48"
(84.46 cm.)   (195.58 cm.)   (121.92 cm.)

PROV. Teina Baumstone, New York.

Another exceedingly rare and important bed, this example and No. 3 are the only two New England, claw-and-ball-footed, low-post beds known to this writer. This is also the only bed yet discovered with open talons on the feet. An unusual feature is the deep indentation of the front of the leg above the foot, providing a strongly muscled appearance to the leg. This peculiarity is also seen on a high chest in the Garvan Collection at Yale.[1] As on No. 1, this example was apparently constructed without knee brackets. Although the bed presents an odd appearance when seen stripped, as here, the absence of brackets is hardly noticeable when the spread is in place. The maker may have decided that they were an extraneous detail.

1952-587

---

1. Carpenter, No. 41.

3. LOW-POST BED

Rhode Island or Massachusetts
1760–90
Mahogany with maple

All parts are mahogany except for the maple rails. The two outside faces of the front posts below the busts are veneered onto the posts themselves (see detail). The left scroll of the headboard is replaced, the left front leg is cracked, and the nose is broken off the left bust. The rails were painted at one time.

H. 37⅜″   L. 76⅜″   W. 59⅜″
  (94.93 cm.)   (194 cm.)   (150.82 cm.)

PROV. J. K. Byard, Norwalk, Conn.; Israel Sack, Inc., New York.

PUBL. *Antiques* 63 (March 1953), p. 262; Alice Winchester, ed., *Antiques Treasury* (New York: E. P. Dutton & Co., 1959), p. 98.

This bed is one of the most unusual examples of its form known and perhaps one of the most significant as well, for it is one of a very small group of pieces of American furniture incorporating sculpture as a decorative motif. Although its history has been lost, the bed has been previously attributed to Newport on the basis of the stop-fluted rear posts and the flat knee carving of the front legs. While the carving is somewhat similar in technique to known Newport work,[1] no exact parallel has been found.

There has also been an attempt to relate the carved heads on the tops of the foot posts to the winged angel heads carved in the spandrels of the built-in cupboards in the Nichols-Wanton-Hunter House in Newport. While a certain simi-

larity in design between the Nichols House angels and the heads on this bed undoubtedly exists, the fact that the bed busts are three dimensional, while the angels are essentially flat and two dimensional, makes it very difficult to compare the two. Spandrel carving of this type was not confined to Newport. Similar heads decorate a cupboard from the William Clough House, which originally stood on Mt. Vernon Place in Boston. The cupboard is presently owned by the Bostonian Society.[2]

Another and perhaps closer comparison can be made between these busts and the known and attributed work of the Skillins of Boston. In particular, the carving here seems related to a bust of Milton on the Moses Brown secretary at the Beverly, Massachusetts, Historical Society.[3] While differences in treatment of the hair and the lower eyelid can be seen, similarities exist as to the arch of the upper eyelid, the eye itself, the small nose, and particularly the enigmatic smile of the mouth. Comparison should also be made to another bust of Milton, part of the original furnishings of the John Brown House;[4] while probably not by Skillin, it also resembles the busts on this bed.

1950-30

---

1. Carpenter, Supplement Nos. 63, 73.

2. Abbott Lowell Cummings, "Decorative Painters and House Painting of Massachusetts Bay, 1630–1725," *American Painting to 1776: A Reappraisal* (Winterthur, Del.: Winterthur Museum, 1971), p. 106.

3. *Antiques* 23 (April 1933), frontis. and p. 142.

4. *John Brown Catalog,* No. 91.

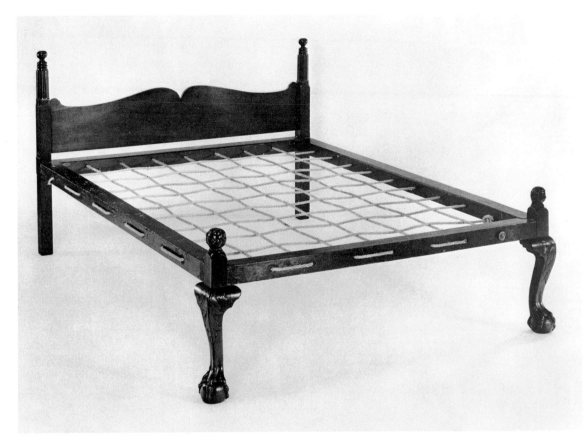

3

3a

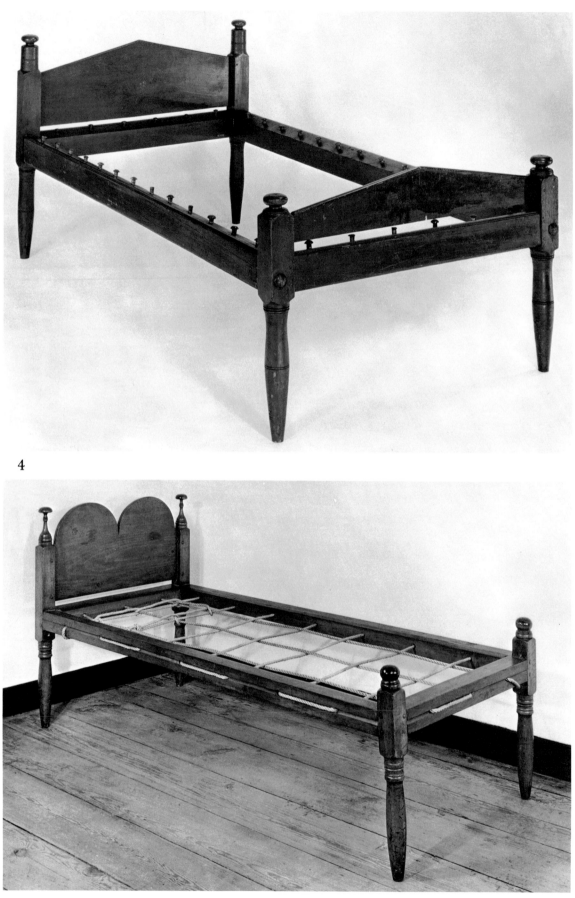

4

5

4 LOW-POST BED
Probably New England
1770–1810
Maple and white pine

The posts and rails are maple; the headboard and footboard are white pine. The rails are attached to the posts with large threaded bolts with screwheads, which are probably not original but have been with the bed for some time. All parts are covered with old, and possibly original, red paint.

H. 33½″   L. 75″   w. 39⅛″
((85.09 cm.)   (190.5 cm.)   (99.38 cm.)

PROV. Mrs. Lawrence J. Ullman, Tarrytown, N.Y.

Although this bed was acquired in New York, the presence of maple and white pine probably indicates a New England origin. The shaping of the posts is similar to that on No. 20, but the ring moldings probably indicate a slightly later date.

1956-200

5 LOW-POST CHILD'S BED
New England
1790–1820
Maple with white pine

The headboard is white pine; all other elements are maple. The surface has been stripped and refinished.

H. 32½″   L. 67½″   w. 29″
(82.55 cm.)   (171.45 cm.)   (73.66 cm.)

PROV. Lillian Blankley Cogan, Farmington, Conn.

Similar in overall design to several eighteenth-century beds in this collection, a later date for this example is suggested by the heavy ring turnings of the legs and the fussy, spindly finials of the head posts.

1950-680

6 TALL-POST BED
Probably Massachusetts or Rhode Island
1740–70
Mahogany, maple, and white pine

The front posts are mahogany, the rear posts and rails are maple, and the headboard is white pine. The left rail was badly twisted when acquired; the tenons have been shaved off and new pieces put in to line up with the mortise holes. Caster holes in the bottom of the posts have been filled in. The mattress is supported on ropes attached to cloth nailed to the inner rebate of the frame.

H. 89½"   L. 76½"   W. 76½"
   (227.33 cm.)   (194.31 cm.)   (194.31 cm.)

PROV.   John S. Walton, Inc., New York.

PUBL.   *Antiques* 100 (August 1971), p. 233.

Cabriole-leg beds with pad feet are extremely rare. Only two other tall-post, New England examples are known—one at Winterthur[1] and one in the collection of Mrs. Walter B. Robb.[2] While all three beds are roughly similar in design, there are significant differences among them. The Winterthur bed is made entirely of maple, Mrs. Robb's bed has walnut foot posts, and this example has foot posts of mahogany. The head posts of the bed at Winterthur are identical to the foot posts, while on the Robb and Williamsburg examples the head posts are simpler and straight. The headboards are alike on all three examples. The form of the front posts is similar on all three beds, with minor differences in the transition between the squared portion at the rail and the cylindrical turning above.

It is in the front legs that the Williamsburg bed seems to differ significantly from the other two examples, which are quite close in design. In both of the other beds the knees are sharp, and the legs terminate in broad, flat pad feet. Scrolled brackets flank the knees on either side. On the Williamsburg bed the knees are rounded, the leg is not as gracefully tapered, and the pad feet sit on very thick discs. Most important, there are no knee brackets nor any evidence of there ever having been any. This is visually disturbing when seen close up, but in the context of the entire bed with its hangings it is hardly noticeable.

The provenance of this bed is open to question. It was acquired indirectly from a dealer in Massachusetts, but has no firm history. Mrs. Robb's bed has a Kingston, Massachusetts, history, and Downs called the Winterthur bed Rhode Island. Without further evidence, it is difficult to pin any of these beds to specific areas, but the use of mahogany here possibly indicates a coastal provenance, and it is likely that all three examples were made somewhere between Boston and Newport.

1959-265

---

1. Downs, No. 1.
2. *Antiques* 92 (September 1967), p. 324.

6

7

8

7 TALL-POST BED
Probably Massachusetts
1760–90
Mahogany with red oak, maple, and white
pine

The foot posts are mahogany, the head posts red oak, all rails and the headboard are maple, and the tester frame is white pine. The headboard has been stained to resemble mahogany, the upper nine inches of each post have been added, and the tester frame is old but probably not original. The left knee bracket of the right front leg is a replacement, the bolt covers are missing, and there is a crack in the ball of the left front foot. The headboard is beaded on the front edge, as are the top outside edges of each rail. The original canvas sacking strips are nailed to the inner edge of three rails and have laced eyelets to receive the rope.

H. 81½"	L. 75"	W. 59½"
(207.01 cm.)	(190.5 cm.)	(151.13 cm.)

PROV. According to tradition, this bed descended in the Potter family of Kingston, R.I.; Harry Arons, Bridgeport, Conn.; R. T. Trump & Co., Inc., Philadelphia.

PUBL. *Antiques* 89 (February 1966), p. 204; 94 (July 1968), p. 58; and 95 (January 1969), p. 95.

On three previous occasions (see above), this bed has been published as the work of a Newport, Rhode Island, craftsman, principally on the basis of the family history and the mistaken assumption that the head posts were chestnut. Comparison with two similar beds attributed to Rhode Island[1] show significant differences, however. On both of these beds the front posts are stop-fluted in the Newport manner and the head posts are octagonal. Most important, both have the high ball and grasping claw so characteristic of Newport workmanship. The bed shown here has none of the above features. The front posts are embellished only with simple flutes, the head posts are square and tapering, and the ball-and-claw feet are flattened with the side claws distinctly raking to the rear. A bed at Winterthur[2] has many of these same attributes, and the canvas sacking to hold the mattress is attached in the same manner.

On this rather limited evidence, this bed is tentatively attributed to Massachusetts. The Kingston, Rhode Island, history cannot be trusted entirely, as another bed in this collection with the same family history (acc. no. 1966-476) is quite definitely a product of Charleston, South Carolina.

1967-530

---

1. *John Brown Catalog*, No. 88, and Carpenter, No. 1. (The latter is better seen in Lockwood II, fig. 806.)
2. Downs, No. 4.

8 TALL-POST BED
Probably New England
1760–90
Mahogany with maple and white pine

The foot posts are mahogany, the rails and head posts are maple, and the headboard is white pine. The slightly arched, moveable headboard is inserted between braces attached to the inside of each head post, rope pegs are attached to the inner rabbeted surface of each rail, the bolt covers and the tester frame are not original, and the knee brackets have been reattached but appear to be original. The bed once had been fitted with a box spring and mattress and the rails contain holes where supporting braces were attached.

H. 88"	L. 78"	W. 59"
(223.52 cm.)	(198.12 cm.)	(149.86 cm.)

PROV. Mrs. J. Insley Blair, New York; Parke-Bernet Galleries, New York.

PUBL. *Important American & English XVIII Century Furniture* (New York: Parke-Bernet Galleries, Inc., January 22, 23, 1954), Lot 166.

Our present lack of knowlege concerning the manufacture of beds of this type makes a definite attribution for this example impossible. The sharp knee and a simple fluting of the front posts indicates a Massachusetts origin, but the high, round feet grasped by long, slender talons are closer to Newport practice. The manner in which the headboard is attached is usually thought to be indicative of Charleston, South

Carolina, but the extensive use of maple in the bed would seem to eliminate that possibility.

The bed is shown standing in the northeast bedroom of the Brush-Everard House in Williamsburg. The hangings are of eighteenth-century blue silk bourette; the coverlet is crewel-embroidered dimity of English origin and dates about 1765.

1954-52

9 TALL-POST BED
Newport, Rhode Island
1760–90
Mahogany with white pine

All elements are mahogany except for the white pine tester frame. The top 10½ inches of each post have been added. Several of the molded strips on the foot posts at the rails have been replaced, and the original bolt covers are missing. A narrow channel, about one-half inch deep, has been cut out of the inside top edge of each rail and has been filled in with new wood and fabric.
H. 87″   L. 74″   w. 55″
   (220.98 cm.)   (187.96 cm.)   (139.70 cm.)

PROV. According to the source from whom this bed was acquired, it came from the Carr House in Newport. Which Carr is unclear, but it may have been the house at 47 Mill Street (formerly Carr's Lane) which was owned by Samuel Carr in 1807 and remained in the family's hands until 1937.[1] John S. Walton, Inc., New York.

PUBL. *Antiques* 95 (January 1969), p. 103.

There seems little question that this bed is a product of Newport craftsmanship. The blocked legs with moldings at the rail and the elaborately scrolled headboard are very similar to the Dennis family bed.[2] The stop-fluting of the front posts above a lamb's-tongue chamfer is a feature

seen on a number of Newport beds, including the fine ball-and-claw-footed example in the John Brown House Show.[3]

1966-197

---

1. Antoinette F. Downing and Vincent I. Scully, Jr., *The Architectural Heritage of Newport, Rhode Island* (New York: Clarkson N. Potter, Inc., 1967), p. 505.
2. Carpenter, No. 3.
3. *John Brown Catalog,* No. 88.

10 TALL-POST BED
Probably Connecticut
1780–1800
Maple with white pine

The posts and rails are maple, the headboard and tester frame white pine. The stamped oval bolt covers appear to be original, and, if so, would necessarily date the bed at the end of the century.
H. 85″   L. 77½″   w. 53″
   (215.90 cm.)   (196.85 cm.)   (134.62 cm.)

PROV. John S. Walton, Inc., New York.

Derived from the same tradition as No. 9, this bed lacks most of its fine details. Missing are the stop fluting of the front posts and the chamfered lamb's-tongue below. The base of the posts are defined only by a simple applied molding. Both the head posts and headboard have lost the graceful lines of the previous example. This deficiency of sophisticated detail does not, in itself, pinpoint the origin of this bed, but combined with the use of native maple rather than the more expensive, imported mahogany, it does indicate a more rural area, possibly Connecticut, as the most likely source.

1966-198

9

10

11

11 TALL-POST BED
Possibly Newport, Rhode Island
1760–90
Mahogany

All elements of the bed are mahogany with the exception of the modern tester frame. The left side rail is cracked at one end. Remnants of old casters are attached to the bottoms of all four feet.

H. 93½"   L. 78"   W. 60"
(237.49 cm.)   (198.12 cm.)   (152.40 cm.)

PROV. Exhibited at the Nichols-Wanton-Hunter House, Newport, 1956. Israel Sack, Inc., New York.

PUBL. *Antiques* 95 (January 1969), p. 96.

The Newport attribution for this bed is hazy, as none of the five related examples known to this writer has a confirmed Newport history. Two of these beds have been attributed to New York. One is very similar to this bed, with the same egg-and-dart molding at the top of the flutes, but in addition, it has carved acanthus leafage above the spiral-turned vase.[1] A second privately owned bed with a history of ownership in New York has the same acanthus leafage, but lacks the egg-and-dart treatment.[2]

A third bed, the most elaborate of the group, has been attributed to Newport on the basis of a vague history in the Ellery and Dennis families of Newport.[3] The faces of the front Marlboro legs are fluted, and all four posts are embellished with molded strips at the rails. The egg-and-dart details are missing, the posts are topped with urn finials, and the headboard is elaborately scrolled. A fourth example is similar to the Carpenter bed, but has the added feature of stop flutes on the front posts.[4]

The Williamsburg bed is, in truth, more similar to the attributed New York examples than to the two attributed to Newport. It may be significant, however, that the spirals on the front posts of this bed swirl in the same direction as those on the Newport beds and counter to those on the two New York examples. Similar spiral turnings are seen on the stair drops at the Nichols-Wanton-Hunter House in Newport. The use of mahogany throughout this bed would also seem to lend credence to a Newport attribution, but a definite statement of provenance is impossible at this time.

1957-34

---

1. *Antiques* 78 (July 1960), p. 17.
2. A photograph of this bed is in the files of Colonial Williamsburg.
3. Carpenter, No. 3.
4. *Sack Brochure 19,* No. P3233.

12 TALL-POST BED
Probably New England
1760–90
Mahogany with maple, white pine, and tulip

The foot posts are mahogany, the head posts and rails are maple, the cornice is white pine, and the headboard is tulip. There are several splits and cracks in both foot posts, the bolt covers are missing, and the present bolts are not original. The painted cornice appears to be original and retains its cream-colored paint and red lower border. The border was once painted green over the red, and traces of the green remain; the bracing strips behind the cornice are not original but are of some age. The headboard is attached to the head posts by means of crude wooden pegs.

H. 90¼″   L. 75¾″   w. 57¼″
  (229.24 cm.)   (192.41 cm.)   (145.41 cm.)

PROV. John S. Walton, Inc., New York.

Very few eighteenth-century American bedsteads with their original painted cornices have survived, but, judging from advertisements of that time, they were apparently quite popular. As early as 1751 a "New Cornish Bedstead" was advertised for sale in New York,[1] and one Minshall, a carver and gilder "from London," advertised in 1769 that he made "bed and window cornicing."[2] The provenance of this particular example is unknown, but the extensive use of maple combined with white pine and tulip suggests a New England origin, perhaps Connecticut or Rhode Island.

1970-147

---

1. *New York Evening Post,* April 8, 1751, as quoted in Rita Susswein Gottesman, *The Arts and Crafts in New York 1726–1776* (New York: New York Historical Society, 1938), p. 123.
2. *New York Journal or the General Advertiser,* December 7, 1769, as quoted in Gottesman, op. cit., p. 128.

13 TALL-POST BED
New England
1810–20
Maple with white pine

The four posts are curly maple, the rails are maple, the headboard and cornice are white pine. The posts, rails, and headboard have been covered with a dark stain; the cornice is painted yellow. The raised panel in the center of each section of the cornice is decorated with a vase of flowers in green, blue-green, red, and gold and is bordered with green striping. The stamped brasses, which show a pair of clasped hands over a branch, appear to be original.

H. 77⅜″   L. 79″   w. 53¾″
  (196.54 cm.)   (200.66 cm.)   (136.55 cm.)

PROV. Philip H. Bradley Co., Downingtown, Pa.

The use of maple in the bed suggests a rural origin, but the superb design and integration of all elements indicates a craftsman well versed in the decorative concepts of the early nineteenth century. The nails used to secure the cornice are of the early cut variety, thus indicating a probable date after 1810, at least for the cornice. The bedhangings of English roller-printed glazed chintz with multicolored flowers on an orange ground have long been with the bed and are possibly original to it. They can be dated between 1798 and 1811.

1967-110

12

13

13a

13b

14

15

14 TALL-POST BED
New England
1760–1810
Maple and white pine

The headboard is white pine; all other elements are maple. The tester frame is modern; the light green paint is old and possibly original.

H. 79¾″   L. 74½″   W. 54¾″
(202.59 cm.)   (189.23 cm.)   (139.09 cm.)

PROV. Israel Sack, Inc., New York.

In 1792 the Hartford, Connecticut, cabinetmakers published a table of prices for cabinetwork. Twenty varieties of bedsteads were listed, including one with "plain square high posts without screws and for a cord with plain tester painted red 1 3 0."[1] This entry almost certainly referred to beds of this type, which could also be made with a sacking bottom (11 shillings extra) and painted green (5 shillings extra). An unusual feature of this example is the manner in which the head posts taper upward in two steps: above the rails the edges are merely chamfered slightly, and the posts do not attain their complete octagonal form until just below the top edge of the headboard.

1951-563

---

1. *The Connecticut Historical Society Bulletin* 33, no. 1 (January 1968), pp. 34–36.

15 TALL-POST BED
New England
1760–1820
Cottonwood, tulip, and maple

The four posts are cottonwood, the rails are maple, and the headboard is tulip. The tester frame is old but not original, and there is an old split in the headboard. The red paint appears to be original.

H. 84″   L. 74¾″   W. 52″
(213.36 cm.)   (189.89 cm.)   (132.08 cm.)

PROV. Roger Bacon Antiques, Exeter, N.H.

On first appearance, most "pencil-post" beds of this type appear to be identical, but there is infinite variety in the small details. On No. 14, the bottom of the posts are square and straight; on this bed they are straight, but octagonal in cross section. Notice also that on the head posts the octagonal form begins just above the rails on the outside of the posts, but the square line is kept on the inside until the top of the headboard.

The use of cottonwood for furniture is rare; at least this writer knows of no other examples. Painted, it resembles maple and birch, and one wonders how many other simple pieces made of this wood have been wrongly identified. A member of the poplar family, it grows principally in the center of this country, and is absent from the eastern coastal plain. Stands are found in Vermont, western Massachusetts, and Connecticut, however, indicating the probable area of production for this bed.

1968-737

16

17

16 TALL-POST BED
Possibly Connecticut
1770–1810
Maple with oak and tulip

The four posts and the side rails are maple, the head and foot rails are oak, the headboard is tulip and is slightly warped. All paint has been removed except from the headboard, which is covered with an old red stain.

H. 71″   L. 73¼″   w. 52½″
  (180.34 cm.)   (186.06 cm.)   (133.35 cm.)

PROV. Roger Bacon Antiques, Exeter, N.H.

Simple beds of this type, embellished only with fluted posts, were probably quite common in the last quarter of the eighteenth century, but few have survived. A birch example at Winterthur is similar, but the posts taper upward directly from the foot and remain square from top to bottom.[1] In this bed, the posts are square at the base but are rounded from the rail up, the transition being eased by lamb's-tongue chamfers at the corners. All surfaces of all four posts are fluted except for the two inner faces of the legs. The deeply scrolled headboard is probably indicative of a comparatively late date. The attribution to Connecticut is based principally on the tulip headboard.

1958-424

---

1. Downs, No. 9

17 TALL-POST BED
Probably Connecticut
1780–1810
Birch and white pine

The headboard and tester frame are white pine; all other elements are birch. The tester frame is old but probably not original. All surfaces are covered with green paint which appears to be mostly original.

H. 82″   L. 78¾″   w. 53¾″
  (208.28 cm.)   (200.05 cm.)   (136.55 cm.)

PROV. J. K. Byard, Norwalk, Conn.

Related to the previous pencil-post examples (Nos. 14–16), the posts here are turned rather than shaped with chamfering or fluting. The bulbous vase at the base of the front posts is reminiscent of that on a Connecticut bed with a Middletown history,[1] but the cylindrical element above and on the head posts is a feature not seen elsewhere.

1951-76

---

1. Kirk, *Connecticut Furniture,* No. 266.

18

19

18 FIELD BED
New England
1780–1820
Maple and white pine

The posts and rails are maple, the headboard and canopy frame white pine. The red paint appears to be mostly original.

H. to top of canopy 80½″   H. of posts 61¼″
      (204.47 cm.)   (155.58 cm.)

L. 76½″   w. 53″
  (194.31 cm.)   (134.62 cm.)

PROV. Israel Sack, Inc., New York.

Another variation of the simple pencil-post bed, here a shortened version with a graceful curved canopy in place of the more common flat, square frame. Here also the legs are straight on their outer surface but tapered on the inner face, lightening the overall effect and perhaps indicating a later date as well.

1953-102

19 FOLDING BED
Possibly Rhode Island
1760–1800
Maple with white pine

The headboard and center supporting legs are white pine. All other elements are maple. The tester frame is a modern replacement. The headboard is old but not original, and a new strip, about 1½ inches in width, has been added at the bottom. Remnants of old green paint are visible on the rails. The headboard is painted red.

H. 74½″   L. 70⅛″   w. 52¾″
 (189.23 cm.)   (178.12 cm.)   (134.01 cm.)

PROV. According to information supplied by the dealer, this bed was "acquired from the Ladd House in Rhode Island." David Stockwell, Inc., Wilmington, Del.

While this folding bed has lost its original headboard and tester frame and is a very plain example, embellished only by the turned knobs on the foot posts and the octagonal shaping of the head posts, it is included here because it represents an obviously important type of eighteenth-century bed of which few complete examples have survived. They could be folded up in the daytime and were obviously useful in small houses with limited floor area.

1954-380

20

21

20 FOLDING BED
New England
1750–1800
Maple and white pine

The headboard and cross brace beneath the bed are white pine; all other elements are maple. Traces of old green paint are visible on the rails. The remainder of the bed is painted red, and this appears to be original.

H. 34¼''　　　L. 77¾''　　　W. 58⅝''
　(87 cm.)　　　(197.49 cm.)　　　(148.91 cm.)

PROV. Israel Sack, Inc., New York.

There is a strong impulse to date folding beds of this type very early in the eighteenth century, but simple examples such as this were almost certainly made and used at least till the end of the century—probably into the nineteenth century as well. The finely beaded outside edges of the rails suggest a date late in the period. The folding front legs are a useful feature not often encountered (see also No. 21).

1966-232

21 FOLDING BED
Probably New England
1780–1820
Maple and white pine

The posts and rails are maple, the headboard white pine. The right head post is split where it joins the rail; the pins in the side rails at the folding joint are replacements. The entire bed is covered with old red paint.

H. 30½''　　　L. 74¼''　　　W. 41¾''
　(77.47 cm.)　　　(188.6 cm.)　　　(106.05 cm.)

PROV. David Stockwell, Inc., Wilmington, Del.

This bed provides an interesting comparison with No. 20. While basically of the same design and form, a later date is indicated by the heavier and more bulbous turnings of the legs and by the different shape of the headboard, with the cut-out semicircles on either side. An interesting structural feature is the thickening of the end and side rails at their juncture with the legs, a sensible strengthening at points that receive a great deal of stress on a bed of this type.

1954-501

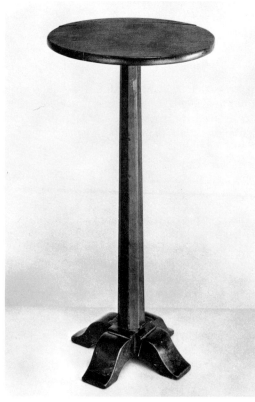

22

PROV. William Wilcox family, Westerly, R.I.; Roger Bacon Antiques, Exeter, N.H.

Stands of this type, usually with elaborate pedestals, are generally credited to Connecticut.[1] A Rhode Island attribution for this example is suggested by its history and by the use of mahogany rather than a native wood such as maple or birch.

1972-304

---

1. Kirk, *Connecticut Furniture,* Nos. 152–53 and Nutting, *Treasury I,* Nos. 1338–39, 1349, 1353–58.

22 CANDLESTAND
Probably Rhode Island
1750–1800
Mahogany and maple

The entire stand is mahogany with the exception of a maple brace beneath the top. The top is stained and split in several places and has been glued and pinned through the side. The brace is attached to the underside of the top by means of six screws, three on each side; all screws are modern and two of the holes appear to be recent additions. The central pillar is doweled into the brace at the top and through the center of the feet at the base. The feet are made in two pieces, one lapped over the other.

H. 24½"   D. of top 14"
  (62.23 cm.)   (35.56 cm.)

23

24

23 CANDLESTAND
New England
1760–90
Mahogany and cherry

The top is mahogany, the pedestal and legs are cherry. The pedestal is doweled into a rectangular block with chamfered edges that is screwed to the underside of the top. The top does not tilt.

H. 28⅛″   TOP 16½″ × 16⅝″
(71.44 cm.)   (41.91 cm. × 42.23 cm.)

PROV. L. G. Myers, New York.

The molded serpentine top and crisp turnings of the pedestal help make this stand one of the most pleasing examples of its type known. The combination of mahogany top with a native wood base, also seen on a dining table in this catalog (No. 136), was apparently a fairly common practice in eighteenth-century New England.

1930-55

24 CANDLESTAND
Probably Massachusetts
1785–1800
Mahogany

All parts are mahogany including the two shaped cleats and turning block on which the top tilts. The triangular catch is brass; beneath the pedestal three iron braces provide reinforcement. The top of the pedestal is slightly cracked.

H. 28¾″   W. 21⅞″   D. 14¾″
(73.05 cm.)   (55.59 cm.)   (37.49 cm.)

PROV. David Stockwell, Inc., Wilmington, Del.

Most stands of this type have legs that terminate in snake feet; few examples are found with carved feet of such delicacy and articulation. The elongated urn shape of the pedestal suggests a date later than the use of ball-and-claw feet might indicate.

1971-387

25

25 CANDLESTAND

Probably Connecticut
1780–1800
Cherry and white pine

The framing and underside of the top and the drawer linings are white pine. The brace beneath the top has been reattached, and the iron brace beneath the pedestal is not original.

H. 25⅝″   w. of top 16¼″   D. of top 16⅛″
  (65.09 cm.)   (41.28 cm.)   (40.96 cm.)

PROV. John S. Walton, Inc., New York.

No other stand of this type has been seen, which is surprising when one considers its utility. The Connecticut attribution is based primarily on the use of cherry.

1971-422

26 CANDLESTAND

Probably Massachusetts
1785–1800
Mahogany

One foot has been broken and repaired; the key holding the bird cage in place is a replacement.
H. 30⅝″   D. of top 20½″
  (77.79 cm.)   (52.07 cm.)

PROV. L. G. Myers, New York.

It is extremely difficult to determine the provenance of small stands of this type, particularly where, as in this case, they are made entirely of mahogany. The spare, slender proportions and the plain, slightly tapering balusters of the bird cage suggest Massachusetts workmanship. Only the urn turning of the pedestal provides a clue to the late date of this stand. The circular, molded top, bird cage, and snake feet are all features commonly found on stands made much earlier in the eighteenth century.

1930-193

27

27 CANDLESTAND
New England
1790–1810
Mahogany

There is a crack in the base of the pedestal; the top has been refinished.

H. 27⅝″   W. 26″   D. 17¾″
(70.17 cm.)   (66.04 cm.)   (45.11 cm.)

PROV. Winick and Sherman, New York.

1930-198

28 CANDLESTAND
New England
1795–1815
Mahogany

Several of the screws securing the braces to the top are replacements. The entire stand has been refinished.

H. 29″   T. 25¾″×16½″
(73.66 cm.)   (65.43 cm. × 41.91 cm.)

PROV. Winick and Sherman, New York.

The heaviness of the pedestal turnings would seem to indicate a relatively late date in the period.

1930-195

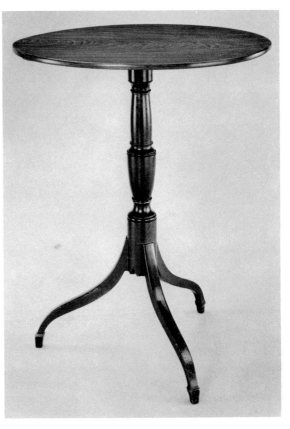

28

29

30

29 ARMCHAIR
Probably southeastern Massachusetts
1640–80
Maple and ash

The four posts and the spindles are maple; the remainder of the chair is ash. Rockers were once attached to the legs, and both front legs have been cut down and spliced above the lower stretchers; the rear legs have been cut down and approximately one-half inch has been added at the bottom. Both front stretchers are replacements, as are the lower stretchers on each side and the center spindle beneath the left arm. The tops of the rear posts have lost their finials, and the mushroom tops of the arm posts are replacements.

H. 42⅛″   w. 25″   D. 17½″
(108.93 cm.)   (63.5 cm.)   (44.45 cm.)

The history of this chair is not known, but it is obviously related to the small group of so-called Carver and Brewster chairs of Plymouth and the surrounding area. While the flattened-ball finials on this chair are generally considered later in date than the more rounded examples, the heaviness and simplicity of the turned elements would seem to indicate a relatively early date. The turnings are close to those on a chair in the Metropolitan Museum, the best preserved of this early type.[1]

Gift of Mrs. Mary M. Sampson,
Wellesley Hills, Mass.
G1942-38, 1

---

1. Nutting, *Pilgrim Century,* fig. 300.

30 ARMCHAIR
Probably Massachusetts
1700–1740
Birch

The chair is constructed entirely of birch. The surface has been scraped, but remnants of red paint remain in some of the crevices. The rush seat is not original.

H. 36⅛″   w. 19⅜″   D. 17⅞″
(91.76 cm.)   (49.22 cm.)   (45.43 cm.)

The narrow ring turnings of the posts, rails, and spindles and the unusual truncated cone feet indicate a very late date for this chair, probably well into the eighteenth century. The use of birch rather than the oak or ash generally used for chairs of this type also suggests this later date, as well as the probability that the chair was made in an area north or west of Boston.

Gift of Mrs. Mary M. Sampson,
Wellesley Hills, Mass.
G1942-38, 3

31

32

31 HIGH CHAIR
Probably Massachusetts
1670–1700
Birch, white oak, walnut, and maple

The posts and the three spindles are birch; the top rail is walnut; the side and rear stretchers, arms, and spindle support are white oak; the two front stretchers are maple and both are probably early replacements, as are the lower rear stretcher and right arm. A footrest was probably originally attached to the front posts where the upper stretcher is now located and was doweled completely through the posts. Most stretchers have been secured with nails of varying antiquity. The rush seat is modern. The feet have probably lost about two inches of height, and the right spindle has been inserted upside down.

H. 34¾″   w. 15″   D. 11″
   (88.29 cm.)   (38.10 cm.)   (27.94 cm.)

Prov. Fred Fuessnich Collection; Israel Sack, Inc., New York.

Few high chairs of this early type are known, and none seen by this author is exactly parallel. The relative simplicity of the turnings probably indicates a date later in the century than one might suspect from the overall style.

1970-113

32 HIGH CHAIR
Probably Massachusetts
1700–1750
Ash and birch

The four posts are ash; the slats, arms, and stretchers are birch. The legs have probably lost about two inches. The lower front stretcher is a replacement, as is the rush seat. The dark red paint appears to be original.

H. 33″   w. 15¼″   D. 11⅝″
   (83.82 cm.)   (38.74 cm.)   (29.53 cm.)

Slat-back high chairs are more common than the spindle-back type, but few are found in as good condition as this small example. The acorn finials suggest a date in the first half of the eighteenth century.

Anonymous gift
G1971-515

33

34

33 ARMCHAIR
New England
1690–1720
Maple and oak

The posts and arms are maple; the stretchers and slats are oak. Approximately one-half inch of the top of the second slat has been broken off, and the top of the left arm post has been repaired. Approximately four inches have been added at the bottom of all four legs. The black paint is old, but not original.

H. 46½" w. 26" D. 17⅝"
(118.11 cm.) (66.04 cm.) (44.77 cm.)

PROV. Roger Bacon Antiques, Exeter, N.H.

Chairs of this form, with downward raking arms and mushroom terminals, are extremely rare. A small group with notched slats, represented at Winterthur, at Bayou Bend, and by an example formerly owned by Mrs. J. Insley Blair,[1] are generally considered the best American chairs of this form. The Williamsburg chair differs from this group in the shaping of the slats, the more rounded finials, and the character of the turnings of the posts. In overall proportion and scale, however, it is a worthy representative of the type.

1971-3309

---

1. Nutting, *Treasury II*, No. 1887.

34 ARMCHAIR
Probably Connecticut
1690–1740
Maple with hickory and ash

The four posts are soft maple, the right arm and slats hickory, and the stretchers ash. The left arm is red oak and is probably a replacement. There has been extensive insect damage to the posts. The top of the bottom slat has been broken off, as has a piece of the inside of the left rear leg at the base. The rush seat is a replacement, and the chair has been stripped and refinished.

H. 39⅛" w. 26" D. 16"
(99.38 cm.) (66.04 cm.) (40.64 cm.)

PROV. Charles Navis, Richmond, Va.

Although a Massachusetts attribution is possible because of the flat, shaped arms and mushroom posts, this chair seems to be associated with a number of examples with strong Connecticut histories. A side chair in the George Dudley Seymour Collection has very similar turnings, finials, and sausage-turned stretchers.[1] That chair came from Newington, as did an armchair of related design in the same collection.[2] Similar feet are found on a chair from Fairfield.[3]

1941-166

---

1. *George Dudley Seymour's Furniture Collection in the Connecticut Historical Society* (Hartford: 1958), No. 75.
2. Ibid., No. 78.
3. Kirk, *Connecticut Furniture*, No. 192.

35

36

35 ARMCHAIR
New England
1690–1740
Maple and oak

The chair is constructed of maple except for oak seat rails and the bottom left stretcher. Both front stretchers, the lower right, and possibly the rear stretcher are replacements. Rockers were once attached to the sides of the legs, and pieces have been inserted to fill in the area cut away. The braided rush seat is old, but not original. Beneath the present black paint are traces of the original red. The arms are turned to complement the turning on the posts.

H. 44¾″   w. 31½″   D. 18⅛″
(113.69 cm.)   (80.01 cm.)   (46.04 cm.)

PROV. Roger Bacon Antiques, Exeter, N.H.

The most striking characteristic of this chair is its unusual width—over five inches wider than No. 34. Because of the width and the slenderness of the slats and arms, the chair appears weak and fragile, an impression that even the bold turnings and generous mushrooms do little to dispel. A chair of similar proportions was found in southern Connecticut.[1]

1972-303

---

1. Nutting, *Pilgrim Century*, No. 364.

36 ARMCHAIR
Massachusetts or Connecticut
1690–1740
Maple and white oak

The front and rear posts are maple, all other elements are white oak. The top slat has lost some of its arch, and the rush seat is a recent replacement. The chair is covered with several coats of red paint over what appears to be the original black.

H. 47″   w. 24⅛″   D. 20⅛″
(119.38 cm.)   (61.28 cm.)   (51.12 cm.)

PROV. Florene Maine, Ridgefield, Conn.

This chair combines elements found in a number of related examples. The front posts are very similar in design to those on a chair at the Museum of Fine Arts in Boston.[1] In the Boston chair, however, the turnings are much crisper and better defined, possibly indicating that the Williamsburg chair is later in date. The turnings of the rear posts resemble those on a baluster-back chair in the Garvan Collection at Yale which by tradition came from Saybrook, Connecticut.[2]

1952-569

---

1. Randall, No. 121.
2. Kirk, *Connecticut Furniture*, No. 200.

37

38

37 ARMCHAIR

Probably Connecticut or Rhode Island
1730–80
Maple and oak

The posts, stretchers, and arms are maple, the slats oak. The legs have been cut down, and there is a possibility the chair once had rockers. The dark red paint is original.

H. 36⅛″   w. 23″   D. 16⅝″
  (91.76 cm.)   (58.42 cm.)   (42.23 cm.)

PROV. Franklin Cushman, Providence, R.I.

This chair was acquired in Rhode Island, but is probably of Connecticut origin. A chair of similar design is in the Garvan Collection at Yale.[1] Several chairs of this same general form, in which the arms do not extend all the way to the front of the seat and are braced by a turned support doweled into a block or swell on the upper side stretcher, are fitted with rockers,[2] and it may well be that this particular form of support was peculiarly adapted to rocking chairs. One such chair, with rockers which appear to be original, has been examined by this writer.

1951-358

---

1. Kirk, *Connecticut Furniture,* No. 196.

2. Nutting, *Pilgrim Century,* Nos. 415–16, and Lockwood II, fig. 425.

38 INVALID CHAIR

New England
1760–1800
Maple and white oak

The chair is constructed entirely of maple with the exception of the three front stretchers, which are of white oak. The chair has lost its original wooden wheels and footrest and has been cut down approximately five inches. The bottom front stretcher is a replacement. The chair is presently covered with black paint under which the original red is visible.

H. 41¼″   w. 21½″   D. 24¼″
  (104.78 cm.)   (54.61 cm.)   (61.60 cm.)

PROV. Stephen Van Rensselaer, Williamsburg, Va.

This chair is virtually identical to a chair in the Salem Towne House at Old Sturbridge Village.[1] The Sturbridge chair is fitted with wooden wheels on the front and rear legs and a footrest at the base of the front and is approximately five inches taller than this example.

William Long, "Cabinet-Maker and Carver from London," working in Philadelphia, advertised in 1785 that he made "Go-Chairs on the newest and best construction, for the ease and comfort of those, who by gout or rheumatic pains, are deprived of the use of their limbs, as they can move themselves from room to room, on one floor, without the assistance of a servant, with ease and expedition...."[2]

1940-18

---

1. Alice Winchester, ed., *Antiques Treasury* (New York: E. P. Dutton & Co., 1959), p. 123.

2. *Pennsylvania Packet,* September 10, 1785, as quoted in Alfred Coxe Prime, *The Arts and Crafts in Philadelphia, Maryland, and South Carolina, 1721–1785* (n.p.: The Walpole Society, 1929), pp. 174–75.

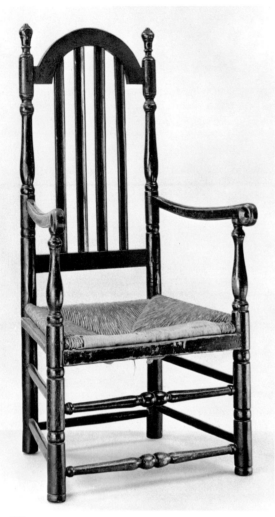

39

40

39 ARMCHAIR
Probably Connecticut
1720–50
Maple

Approximately three inches have been pieced onto the bottom of all four legs. Four strips of white pine have been nailed to the legs beneath the seat as a reinforcement; these strips were probably added in the nineteenth century. The second slat from the left in the back is a modern replacement, and the buttons have been lost from the finials. The rush seat is old and has been patched at the front. The black paint is old and, for the most part, appears to be original.

H. 47″   W. 24¼″   D. 18″
  (119.38 cm.)   (61.60 cm.)   (45.72 cm.)

PROV. Roger Bacon Antiques, Exeter, N.H.

The only other similar chair found appears to have thinner and less well defined turnings, and the crest of the back is not as highly arched.[1] Although no history accompanies the chair, most reeded or grooved banister-back chairs have Connecticut histories.[2] The unusual holes in the arm terminals may have been designed for a restraining bar, but as there is little evident wear, they were probably intended as merely decorative devices.

1972-305

1. Nutting, *Pilgrim Century,* No. 538.
2. Kirk, *Connecticut Furniture,* Nos. 204–14.

40 SIDE CHAIR
Massachusetts, Boston area
1720–60
Maple with red oak

The seat rails and lower back rail are red oak; the rest of the chair is maple. Both the back and the seat have been reupholstered. The cresting rail is cracked above the right stile and the right front leg has been repaired above the foot. The chair has been stained black in this century. The toes of the front feet are made separately and applied, as is usual in chairs of this type.

The figures *IIII* in chalk appear on the right seat rail.

H. 45″   W. 18″   D. 14¾″
  (114.30 cm.)   (45.72 cm.)   (37.47 cm.)

PROV. Henry A. Hoffman, Litchfield, Conn.

Chairs of this type were made in Boston and probably in other coastal areas of New England during much of the second and third quarters of the eighteenth century. They were widely exported and were known as "Boston" or "New England" chairs. Almost invariably made of maple and upholstered in leather, they had either an undulating crest—as on this example—or a rounded one, and either Spanish or small button feet. They appear quite commonly in Philadelphia inventories of the period and in Maryland and Virginia records as well. Thomas Latimer of Westmoreland County, Virginia, owned "12 New England chairs" in 1746.[1]

1952-265

1. The definitive article on this particular variety of seat furniture is Richard H. Randall, Jr., "Boston Chairs," *Old-Time New England* 54 (Summer 1963), pp. 12–20.

41

42

41 SIDE CHAIR
New England
1730–1800
Maple with beech

The seat frame of this chair has been identified as beech, a rare occurrence of this wood in American furniture. There is a small crack on the left side of the cresting rail and another on the left rear leg. The chair was painted black at one time. When acquired, the seat was partly covered with old, and possibly original, leather.

H. 41½″   W. 18½″   D. 15¼″
(105.41 cm.)   (46.99 cm.)   (38.74 cm.)

PROV. John S. Walton, Inc., New York.

This chair is closely related to the previous example, differing only in the shaping of the crest rail and the substitution of a vase-shaped splat for the upholstered rectangular back. It seems probable that chairs of both types were produced at approximately the same time, the customer dictating which form he desired. An early date is often given to these chairs, which were widely produced throughout New England, because of the retention of the blocked and baluster-turned legs and stretchers and Spanish feet. But almost certainly this type was made well into the eighteenth century and possibly as late as 1800. That this particular example may be one of the later productions is indicated by the squat nature of the turnings and the very coarse and ill-defined feet.

1959-101

42 SIDE CHAIR
New England
1730–80
Maple

Remnants of the original red stain are visible beneath the present dark finish. A small piece is broken off the lower right edge of the splat. The rush seat is a replacement.

H. 41½″   W. 20″   D. 15¼″
(105.41 cm.)   (50.80 cm.)   (38.74 cm.)

PROV. John S. Walton, Inc., New York.

This chair is an unusual and rather sophisticated variant on the preceding example. The shape of the back and of the splat is very close to No. 48 with the exception of the treatment of the base. The compass rush seat with the exposed corners is unusual but visually very pleasing, following as it does the curvilinear outline of the back. The treatment of the base is similar to both of the previous chairs except at the top of the front legs, where an elongated thimble element has been substituted for the normal rectangular block. While chairs of this general form were made throughout New England, this particular variation, utilizing relatively sophisticated motifs, was probably made in one specific geographical area. An identical pair, possibly made in the same shop, was owned in 1962 by Israel Sack, Inc.[1]

1959-102

---

1. *Sack Brochure 9,* No. 483.

43

44

43 ARMCHAIR
Probably Massachusetts or New Hampshire
1730–80
Maple

The chair has been stained dark, probably in this century. The feet have been worn considerably, and there is a repair at the point where the left arm joins the back. The front stretcher has been turned. The rush seat is a replacement.

H. 40¾″   W. 22½″   D. 16⅞″
(103.53 cm.)   (57.15 cm.)   (42.89 cm.)

PROV. George Kernodle, Washington, D.C.

Another variant on the same basic form as the previous chairs, this example is virtually identical to No. 41 but has been broadened to compensate for the addition of arms. The rush seat was much more commonly used on these chairs than the stuffed and upholstered seats. A very similar example was owned by Israel Sack, Inc., in 1961.[1]

1952-346

---

1. *Sack Brochure 7,* No. 375.

44 ARMCHAIR
Probably Massachusetts
1725–50
Walnut

The old slip-seat frame is maple, and there are no corner blocks. A thin split runs along the outside edge of the left arm at the rear.

H. 43⅛″   W. 22″   D. 15¾″
(109.54 cm.)   (55.88 cm.)   (40.01 cm.)

PROV. Ginsburg and Levy, New York.

This chair carries the stylistic progression of the preceding examples one step further. The arms and arm supports are closely related to those on the previous chair, but are more skillfully designed and better executed. With the exception of these features and the square seat, the chair is entirely in the accepted Queen Anne style and is close in overall design to Nos. 47 through 50.

1970-103

45

46

45 SIDE CHAIR
New England
1760–1800
Maple

The chair has been stripped and refinished, but remnants of the original greenish-black paint remain. The rush seat is a replacement.

H. 39⅜″   w. 20½″   D. 18″
(100.02 cm.)   (52.07 cm.)   (45.72 cm.)

Although later in style (if not in actual date) than the preceding examples, this chair is included here because of the obvious relationship in overall design. The back and splat have assumed the rectilinear character of the later Chippendale style, but the legs, stretchers, and seat retain the much earlier features. Variations of this chair were made for many years throughout New England.[1] The unusual turnings of the front and side stretchers may eventually permit this particular variant to be assigned to a specific geographical area.

Gift of the estate of Mrs. Ernest J. Hanford.
G1965-111

---

1. For similar examples see *New Hampshire Arts,* figs. 26 and 27; Lockwood II, fig. 539; Nutting, *Treasury II,* Nos. 2097 and 2098; and Charles S. Bissell, *Antique Furniture in Suffield, Connecticut, 1670–1835* (Hartford: Connecticut Historical Society and Suffield Historical Society, 1956), pl. 12.

46 ARMCHAIR
Probably Connecticut
1780–1830
Maple with tulip and ash

All elements are maple with the exception of the tulip splat and bottom rail and the ash front and lower side stretchers. The chair is covered with old red paint which appears to be original. Two inches have been added to the base of the rear feet. The front stretcher is split slightly.

H. 43⅛″   w. 23¾″   D. 17½″
(109.54 cm.)   (60.32 cm.)   (44.45 cm.)

PROV. Charles Navis, Richmond, Va.

How this chair fits into the preceding group is difficult to determine. It is certainly related in the overall design of the back, in the baluster arm supports, and the baluster-and-ring front stretcher. However, each of these features is designed apart from the others; there is no integration among the various elements. Some parts, notably the cresting rail, are very pinched and weak. Others, such as the flaring arms and the front stretcher, are exaggerated almost to comic proportions. The inevitable conclusion must be that this chair is a very late and degenerate version of the earlier style, most likely made in the first quarter of the nineteenth century. Chairs of this general design were made in both New York and Connecticut, and it is impossible to pinpoint this particular example.[1]

1939-277

---

1. A related "Dutch chair" is pictured in Nutting, *Treasury II,* No. 2107. A Connecticut example with a similar front stretcher is pictured in Kirk, *Connecticut Furniture,* No. 223.

47

47 SIDE CHAIR
Massachusetts
1730–70
Walnut

There are no secondary woods in the chair itself; the slip-seat frame is maple and has been with the chair for some time but is probably not original. There is an old break on the upper edge of the left seat rail which has been skillfully repaired. The upper left side of the splat has been pieced. The inside of the front seat rail is straight, forming the slip seat support.

The chair is numbered *V* on the inside of the front seat rail. The slip seat is numbered *III*.

H. 41″   w. 19⅞″   D. 16¾″
(104.14 cm.)   (50.51 cm.)   (42.57 cm.)

PROV.   L. G. Myers, New York.

This is the classic New England chair of the Queen Anne period and embodies all of the essential elements of the design: the tall, slender back with flat stiles, the yoke cresting rail, balloon seat, plain cabriole front legs terminating in cushioned pad feet, and blocked-and-turned stretchers. The craftsman has subtly succeeded in lightening the mass of the chair by scraping out the bottom of the seat frame on the front and sides and chamfering the rear legs. Very similar chairs are found in a number of public and private collections. A set of six chairs in the Garvan Collection at Yale belonged to President Holyoke of Harvard.[1] A single chair at the Museum of Fine Arts in Boston differs only in the lack of ring turnings on the medial and rear stretchers,[2] as does a pair that descended in the Pierce family of Portsmouth, New Hampshire.[3]

1930-164

1. Kirk, *Chairs*, No. 101
2. Randall, No. 134
3. *Sack Brochure 3*, No. 120

PEYTON RANDOLPH HOUSE, West Bedroom

*HIGH CHEST OF DRAWERS, Connecticut, Southbury area,
attributed to a member of the Booth family, 1780–1800. (No. 82).*

48 SIDE CHAIR
Massachusetts or Rhode Island
1730–70
Walnut

There is a small crack in the front seat rail above the left front leg. The slip-seat frame is maple and may be original to the chair.

VI cut into the inside of seat rail and on the slip-seat frame.

H. 39⅛″   D. 16⅞″   w. 21⅝″
  (99.38 cm.)   (42.89 cm.)   (54.93 cm.)

PROV. L. G. Myers, New York.

PUBL. *Girl Scouts,* No. 572.

One of a pair in this collection, the other chair is numbered *IIII* both on the seat rail and slip-seat frame. Only slight differences separate this example from the previous chair. The splat has been cut out and lightened at the top, and the feet are broader and flatter and lack (or have lost) the high pad of the preceding example. The rear legs have been cut back at the base to further lighten the bulk.

The hazards of attributing any of these chairs to a specific locality is evidenced by comparing this chair with an example at Winterthur which is attributed to Newport on the basis of a carved shell in the center of the cresting rail.[1] With the exception of this detail, the two chairs are virtually identical.

1930-222

48

1. Downs, No. 101

49

50

49   SIDE CHAIR
Massachusetts or Rhode Island
1750–80
Mahogany

The slip-seat frame in this chair and its mate (also in the Colonial Williamsburg collection) are maple. Both frames are old, but probably not original.

III carved into the inside front seat rail. *VI* carved into matching chair.

H. 40″   w. 20¼″   D. 17⅛″
  (101.60 cm.)   (51.44 cm.)   (43.50 cm.)

PROV.   L. G. Myers, New York.

PUBL.   *Girl Scouts,* No. 571.

The variations on this standard New England type seem endless. From the crest rail to the ankles, this chair could be a mate to No. 47, but in place of the usual flat pads, the craftsman has chosen to terminate the legs in knuckly ball-and-claw feet. On viewing this feature, one is tempted to consider the chair a transitional example between the Queen Anne and the later Chippendale styles, but the evidence is increasingly clear that simple chairs of this type could be ordered with either foot treatment, and thus it is impossible to assign a date on the basis of the foot design. The provenance of this chair has been the subject of some discussion. The overall design and proportions indicate a Massachusetts origin, but the almost square, knuckly foot with a prominent web between the talons is closer in design to similar features on both Rhode Island and New York furniture.[1] An identical pair, numbered *I* and *IV,* was owned in 1961 by Ginsburg and Levy of New York.

1930-165, 2

---

1. Kirk, *Chairs,* Nos. 131 and 168.

50   SIDE CHAIR
Massachusetts, Boston area
1730–70
Walnut

The slip-seat frame is of soft maple and appears to be original. The triangular corner blocks are walnut, but are not original. A series of unexplained holes has been drilled through all four seat rails, and some have been partially filled in. The rear knee bracket of the left front leg has been cracked and repaired. The front bracket on the left leg is a replacement. The right front leg has been repaired where it joins the side stretcher.

XI (or *IX*) cut into front seat rail and slip-seat frame; *V* cut into top and bottom of left front corner block.

H. 39¼″   w. 19¾″   D. 16¼″
  (99.70 cm.)   (50.19 cm.)   (41.28 cm.)

PROV.   Mrs. J. Wiederspohn, Camden, N.J.

Similar in design to Nos. 47 through 49, this chair incorporates a number of refinements. The rear legs are cylindrical in shape for much of their length, a characteristic seen on several similar Rhode Island chairs.[1] The scalloping of the front rail further lightens the overall effect. This particular pattern seems to have been quite popular, as a large number of virtually identical examples are known. A set of six with a Boston history was owned at one time by Israel Sack, Inc.[2] A set of four was included in the Philip Flayderman Collection[3] and a pair in the collection of Francis P. Garvan.[4] Other examples are currently in the collections of Old Sturbridge Village[5] and the Museum of Fine Arts in Boston.[6] The Sturbridge chair is branded *J. Langdon* and belonged to the Ellery family of Gloucester; the MFA chair has a Boston history.

1970-105

---

1. *John Brown Catalog,* Nos. 2 and 3.
2. *Antiques* 51 (June 1947), p. 355.
3. *Colonial Furniture, Silver & Decorations* (New York: American Art Association, Anderson Galleries, Inc., January 2, 3, 4, 1930), Lot 499.
4. *Furniture and Silver by American Master Craftsmen of Colonial and Early Federal Times* (New York: American Art Association, Anderson Galleries, Inc., January 8, 9, 10, 1931), Lot 388.
5. Kirk, *Chairs,* No. 99.
6. Randall, No. 135.

51 SIDE CHAIR
Newport, Rhode Island
1740–70
Walnut

The slip-seat frame is maple. There are no corner blocks in the seat frame. The shell is not applied, but carved from the crest rail. The splat is chamfered on the rear edges to lighten the mass.

VI cut into the inside of front seat rail; *V* cut into slip-seat frame.

H. 41″	w. 21″	D. 17⅛″
(104.14 cm.)	(53.34 cm.)	(43.50 cm.)

PROV. L. G. Myers, New York.

PUBL. *Girl Scouts,* No. 569; Marion Day Iverson, *The American Chair* (New York: Hastings House, 1957), fig. 57; Milo M. Naeve, "The American Furniture," *Antiques* 95 (January 1969), p. 132.

Few pieces of furniture are visually as satisfying as this superb chair. A study in the use of curves, the flowing surfaces are broken only by the straight lines of the stretchers and rear legs. From the seat down, the chair is virtually identical to No. 48, but above the seat the chair takes on an entirely different character with its rounded stiles, flowing vase-shaped splat, and carved shell at the center of the crest rail. Few New England chairs with rounded stiles have survived, and most of these are associated with Newport.[1] Closest in design to the Williamsburg example is a set of four chairs at the Moses Brown School in Providence,[2] attributed to John Goddard on the basis of a letter from Moses Brown to Goddard dated 1763. While not identical in all respects (the splat is narrower and the transition between the stiles and back legs is more abrupt), the similarities in design and in the carving of the shell indicate possible production by the same craftsman. Another very similar pair with a matching slipper chair was owned by Israel Sack, Inc., in 1971.[3]

1930-158

---

1. Kirk, *Chairs,* Nos. 161–66.
2. Ibid., No. 163.
3. *Sack Brochure 20,* Nos. P3318, P3319.

52 SIDE CHAIR
Newport, Rhode Island
1735–60
Mahogany

The slip-seat frame is maple; there are no corner blocks. The C scrolls flanking the legs are not applied but are carved from the solid block of the leg. The volutes at the base of the scrolls run completely behind the leg. The very thick splat is chamfered slightly on the edges to lighten its appearance. The crest rail has been repaired where it joins both stiles. Approximately one inch has been added to the base of the rear legs.

III carved into inside of front rail and into slip-seat frame.

H. 42″	w. 20½″	D. 16½″
(106.68 cm.)	(52.07 cm.)	(41.91 cm.)

PROV. Israel Sack, Inc., New York.

PUBL. *Sack Brochure 14,* No. 914.

Chairs of this type with flat stretchers have been attributed to Newport since the sale of a set of six chairs in the Philip Flayderman Collection in 1930.[1] These chairs, which appear to differ from the Williamsburg example only in the shaping of the seat rail, were said to have been made by Job Townsend, although supporting evidence has never been published. Similar chairs with straight seat rails are at the Newport Historical Society, at Winterthur,[2] and in a private collection.[3] The only other example with a shaped skirt was exhibited in the John Brown House show in 1965.[4] On the basis of a photograph, it appears to be identical to this example in all respects with the exception of being made of walnut rather than mahogany.

1970-102

---

1. *Colonial Furniture, Silver & Decorations* (New York: American Art Association, Anderson Galleries, Inc., January 2, 3, 4, 1930), Lot 492.
2. *Antiques* 98 (December 1970), p. 903.
3. Carpenter, No. 13.
4. *John Brown Catalog,* No. 4.

51

52

53

54

54a

53 SIDE CHAIR
Probably Massachusetts
1765–90
Walnut

The slip-seat frame of this chair and that of its mate are walnut. The chair was made without corner blocks, although triangular blocks have been added at a later date.

V carved into inside of front seat rail and on slip seat (*II* carved on other chair in collection).

H. 38¼″   w. 20⅜″   D. 17″
   (97.16 cm.)   (51.76 cm.)   (43.18 cm.)

PROV. Mrs. W. S. Ahern, Richmond, Va.

These chairs were acquired in Richmond, Virginia, over thirty years ago, but are quite definitely not southern. Similar chairs have turned up in Massachusetts, notably in the Boston area. A set of similar design, upholstered over the seat rails, once belonged to Governor Elbridge Gerry; these chairs are now in the Old State House in Boston.[1] Three very similar examples, branded *E. Stephenson,* were in the collection of Blin W. Page.[2] Two related chairs are at the Museum of Fine Arts in Boston. One with a pierced splat retains its original needlework seat worked in Brookline, Massachusetts, about 1776.[3] It was also made originally without corner blocks. The second chair is similar in design to the Williamsburg chair but has pointed knees.[4] The front legs of both of the Boston Museum chairs terminate in pad feet on deep, wide cushions identical to those on the Williamsburg chair. Randall speculates that this pad is not a truly Queen Anne feature, but that the large pad was the block left by the maker to carve either this foot or a ball-and-claw foot, as the customer wished. The same foot is also seen on the following chair.

1939-102, 1

---

1. Esther Singleton, *Furniture of our Forefathers, Part IV* (New York: Doubleday, Page, & Co., 1901), p. 276.

2. *Fine American XVIII Century Furniture* (New York: Parke-Bernet Galleries, Inc., January 26, 27, 1945), Lot 232.

3. Randall, No. 147.

4. Randall, No. 153.

54 SIDE CHAIR
Massachusetts, Boston or North Shore
1760–90
Mahogany with white pine

The triangular corner blocks are white pine, and each is attached with two rose-headed nails. The maple slip-seat frame is old, but probably not original. The upper half of each stile is rounded on the back, the lower half is chamfered. The seat rails are of unusual thickness and are molded on the upper, outside edges; there is a split across the right side of the front seat rail.

IIII cut into inside of front seat rail. *VI* is carved into slip-seat frame.

H. 38½″   w. 21½″   D. 17⅜″
   (97.79 cm.)   (54.61 cm.)   (44.14 cm.)

PROV. This chair descended in the Dane family of Andover, Massachusetts, along with No. 55; Roland B. Hammond, Inc., North Andover, Mass.

Endless variations of chairs with this splat design were made in Massachusetts during the Chippendale period. A set of six without carving, but similar in other details, was owned by Israel Sack, Inc., in 1970.[1] An example with a fluted shell and ball-and-claw feet was in the Girl Scout Loan Exhibition,[2] and a pair with similar, but not identical, carved crest rails was also owned by Israel Sack, Inc.[3] The cushioned pad feet on this chair are even more exaggerated than those on the previous example and are further emphasized by the unusual scored lines. While it is possible that the lines were added at a later date, this writer has seen several other Massachusetts chairs of the period with similar embellishments. (This feature can be seen on a set of very unusual chairs that descended in the Winslow Warren family of Massachusetts.[4]) The squared rear legs are frequently found on Massachusetts chairs without stretchers.

1970-130

---

1. *Sack Brochure 18,* No. 1386.

2. *Girl Scouts,* No. 604.

3. *Sack Brochure 14,* No. 875.

4. *Sack Brochure 19,* No. P3250.

55

55 SIDE CHAIR
Salem, Massachusetts
1765–80
Mahogany with maple and white pine

The large, triangular corner blocks are of white pine and are nailed to the frame. The rear blocks have been reattached. The front leg carries up through the maple seat rails and projects upward at the corner above the level of the rails. The splat has cracked and been repaired at the center right and the feet have small cracks. The small mahogany brackets between the seat rails and rear legs are covered when the chair is upholstered.

H. 37⅜″   W. 20⅜″   D. 17½″
 (94.94 cm.)   (51.76 cm.)   (44.45 cm.)

PROV. This chair descended in the Dane family of Andover, Massachusetts, with chair No. 54; Roland B. Hammond, Inc., North Andover, Mass.

55a

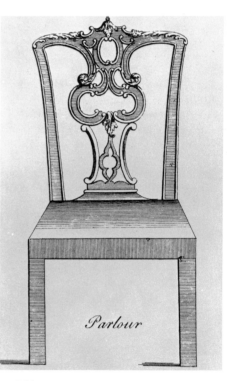

Parlour

55b

The splat design of this chair was taken from Robert Manwaring, *The Cabinet and Chair-Maker's Real Friend and Companion* (London, 1765), pl. 9 (see detail). Several sets of chairs from the Salem area utilizing the design are known. The Williamsburg example is apparently part of the same set as a chair in the Massachusetts Historical Society with the same knee carving against a punched ground (see detail). A very closely related set, differing only in the depth of the knee carving and lacking the punched ground, is represented by chairs at the Essex Institute in Salem,[1] the Museum of Fine Arts in Boston,[2] and Winterthur.[3] The Winterthur chair has an inscription inside the front seat rail which reads *Bottum'd June 1773 by WVE Salem.* A more elaborate chair of the same design but with a carved cresting rail and splat descended in the Pickman family of Salem.[4]

Anonymous gift
G1970-132

1. Fales, *Essex County Furniture,* No. 55.
2. Randall, No. 144.
3. Kirk, *Chairs,* No. 113.
4. Ibid., No. 114.

56

56 SIDE CHAIR

Massachusetts, Salem area
1770–1800
Mahogany with maple and white pine

This chair is one of a pair in the Colonial Williamsburg collection. The seat rails are maple, the original triangular corner blocks white pine. The chair has been upholstered a number of times as is evidenced by several rows of tack holes on the rails and legs.

H. 38″   w. 20¾″   D. 19¾″
   (96.52 cm.)   (52.73 cm.)   (50.19 cm.)

PROV. Willis Stallings, High Point, N.C.

A number of chairs of this pattern are known in the Salem area, and they were probably made there. The source of the design of the back is the same as that of No. 54, but the undulating cresting rail, which flows into the top of the stiles, is similar to that on the preceding chair, also from Salem. This chair, along with its mate, was discovered in eastern North Carolina, and other chairs of the same pattern have turned up in that area, perhaps indicating that simple chairs of this type were a common export item of Salem makers.

1963-40, 2

57

58

57 SIDE CHAIR
Connecticut or Rhode Island
1770–1800
Mahogany with maple and chestnut

The rear seat rail and slip-seat frame are maple; the open diagonal corner blocks are chestnut and have been nailed several times, but the old nail holes match up with those in the seat frame, and the blocks appear to be original. The rear surfaces of the stiles are rounded as are the top edges of the seat rails. The mate to this chair is also in the Williamsburg collection.

III cut inside of front seat rail; *VI* cut into slip-seat frame (matching chair numbered *IIII* on both seat rail and slip-seat frame; *Talbut* in chalk on chair 2).

H. 38″   w. 21″   D. 17″
(96.52 cm.)   (53.34 cm.)   (43.18 cm.)

Chairs of this pattern are generally attributed to Rhode Island,[1] but most Rhode Island examples have a cross-hatched cresting rail, a carved splat, and stop-fluted front legs. The simplicity of the execution of this chair, with its simple "soft" shell, undecorated splat, and molded legs, suggests the hand of a rural craftsman working within the sphere of influence of Rhode Island. While the pattern is not common in Connecticut, at least one similar chair, with a Seymour family history, is known.[2] In addition, a chair which appears identical to the Williamsburg chair in all respects was owned in 1928 by Henry Wood Erving of Hartford.[3]

Gift of the estate of Mrs. Ernest J. Hanford.
G1965-106, 1.

---

1. *John Brown Catalog,* No. 12. *Antiques* 97 (January 1970), p. 82.
2. Connecticut Historical Society, *Connecticut Chairs* (Hartford: 1956), pp. 46–47.
3. Nutting, *Treasury II,* No. 2267.

58 SIDE CHAIR
Probably Connecticut, New Britain or
    Farmington area
1770–88
Cherry with oak

The slip-seat frame is made of cherry and oak and appears to be original. The corner blocks are replacements, the right rear leg is cracked at the seat rail and stretcher, and the right front leg is cracked on the outside.

VIII cut into inside of front seat rail and slip-seat frame.

H. 38″   w. 18½″   D. 15⅛″
(96.52 cm.)   (46.99 cm.)   (38.42 cm.)

PROV. This chair was apparently owned by John and Ruth (Stanley) Mix of New Britain and Farmington, Connecticut. John Mix was born in New Haven and married (date unknown) Ruth Stanley, daughter of Deacon Noah Stanley of New Britain. She was born on July 15, 1756, and died in New Haven in 1811. The date of her husband's death is unknown. Portraits of Mr. and Mrs. Mix, painted in 1788, are in the Abby Aldrich Rockefeller Folk Art Collection in Williamsburg. The chair descended with the portraits and is thought to be the one (or one of the same set) in which both subjects are seated.[1] Ginsburg and Levy, New York.

The extreme simplicity and rather crude character of this chair points to a rural provenance, and it seems likely the chair was made in the New Britain-Farmington area southwest of Hartford. The squared, scrolled ear is seen on some simple New York chairs, while the splat design was popular throughout the New England and New York areas. A similar, slightly more sophisticated, chair was made in Fairfield, Connecticut, by David Bulkley.[2]

1941-74

---

1. Nina Fletcher Little, *The Abby Aldrich Rockefeller Folk Art Collection* (Williamsburg, Va.: Colonial Williamsburg, 1957), figs. 10, 11.
2. Kirk, *Connecticut Furniture,* No. 240.

59

60

59 SIDE CHAIR
Probably Rhode Island
1790–1800
Mahogany with maple and white pine

The seat rails are soft maple, the open diagonal corner braces white pine. The lower left corner of the splat has been broken and repaired.

H. 38″   W. 21″   D. 19¼″
  (96.52 cm.)   (53.34 cm.)   (48.90 cm.)

Chairs of this type were made in both Rhode Island and Connecticut and possibly in other areas of New England as well. Examples are known in cherry, birch, and mahogany, and slight variations in splat design occur. This particular chair is the only one observed in which the central piercing of the bottom of the splat has a convex lower edge. As this example is made of mahogany and most documented Connecticut examples are of cherry, a tentative Rhode Island attribution is called for.[1]

Gift of the estate of Mrs. Ernest J. Hanford.
G1965-108

---

1. For similar examples see Montgomery, No. 41; *John Brown Catalog,* No. 16; Connecticut Historical Society, *Connecticut Chairs* (Hartford: 1956), pp. 48–49.

60 CORNER CHAIR
Probably Massachusetts
1760–90
Mahogany with maple

The rear rails are of maple, faced on the exterior with mahogany. The four triangular corner blocks are also maple and have been attached to the chair for some time, but may not be origi- nal. The arm rail has been broken and pieced at the center, the left knee is cracked and has been repaired, the front leg has been repaired as has the left knee bracket, which has been reinforced with a screw. The bottom of all four feet have been cut down slightly and casters were once attached. The slip-seat frame is not original.

III carved into left front seat rail.

H. 31″   W. 26¼″   D. 26⅛″
  (78.74 cm.)   (66.68 cm.)   (66.36 cm.)

PROV. L. G. Myers, New York.

PUBL. *Girl Scouts,* No. 610.

This is one of the most elaborate New England corner chairs known and one of the most puzzling as well, for its origin is difficult to determine. The broad, pierced splats are unlike those found on any other chair known to this writer, but in the details and method of execution, they are close to Massachusetts splats of the period (see No. 54). A similar, shaped cresting rail and fluted columnar supports can be seen on a chair attributed to Salem.[1] The sharp knees of this chair are also characteristic of Massachusetts seat furniture, but the high, square feet with the prominent web between the knuckles are much more typical of New York or Rhode Island workmanship, and the lack of stretchers is uncharacteristic of Massachusetts during this period. The weight of this evidence seems to indicate Massachusetts as the most likely origin, but the possibility of a Rhode Island attribution must be considered.

1930-160

---

1. Sack, *Fine Points,* No. 74.

61

62

61 BACK STOOL
Probably Massachusetts
1770–1800
Mahogany with maple and white pine

The seat rails and back framing are maple; two triangular corner blocks of white pine are nailed inside the front corners of the seat frame and appear to be original. There is no evidence of blocks at the rear corners. All four legs have been pieced approximately one inch at the base, and the legs have been refinished.

H. 38″	W. 22½″	D. 20¼″
(96.52 cm.)	(57.15 cm.)	(51.44 cm.)

PROV. Williams Antique Shop, Old Greenwich, Conn.

The back stool was apparently never as popular in America as it was in England, for few examples have survived, and eighteenth-century documentation for their use is scanty. The earliest eighteenth-century reference to the term "back stool" for an armless chair with upholstered seat and high back was apparently in Ince and Mayhew's *The Universal System of Household Furniture,* plates 55 and 56, published in London between 1759 and 1762. That the chairs were in use in America in the 1760s is confirmed by visual evidence in paintings—for instance, Copley's portrait of Daniel Hubbard painted in 1764[1]—but no written reference to the term has been seen earlier than a 1772 advertisement by Richard Fowler of Charleston who gave notice that he "carries on the upholsterer's business...such as...French Elbow Chairs, French Back-Stools. . . ."[2] In 1774 Charles Allen of Philadelphia, "Lately from London and Paris &c," advertised that he made "stuff sofas, settees, couches, French elbow, easy, corner and backstool chairs...."[3] An unusual feature of this chair is that no brackets were ever attached beneath the seat rail on the sides. The upholstery is a blue-and-white resist fabric.

1951-399

1. Jules D. Prown, *John Singleton Copley,* 2 vols. (Cambridge: Harvard University Press, 1966), vol. 1, fig. 138.
2. *South Carolina Gazette,* May 21, 1772, as quoted in Alfred Coxe Prime, *The Arts and Crafts in Philadelphia, Maryland, and South Carolina 1721–1785* (n.p.: The Walpole Society, 1929), p. 203.
3. *Pennsylvania Packet,* September 5, 1774, quoted in Prime, op. cit., p. 200.

62 BACK STOOL
Probably Newport, Rhode Island
1770–1800
Mahogany with maple and white pine

The seat rails and back frame are soft maple. Two original, very large corner blocks of white pine are nailed and glued to the seat frame, the other two blocks are missing. The rear legs are spliced at an angle to the back posts above the rear seat rail, both front legs are split from top to bottom, and the lower back brace is a replacement.

H. 38″	W. 21″	D. 17¾″
(96.52 cm.)	(53.34 cm.)	(45.11 cm.)

PROV. John S. Walton, Inc., New York.

No other American back stool with stop-fluted front legs is known to this writer. While stop-fluting was used as a decorative embellishment in other areas of America, it was most commonly found in Rhode Island work. Unusual for Newport, however, is the molding of the side and medial stretchers in the same manner as No. 61.

1968-805

63

63 UPHOLSTERED ARMCHAIR
Probably Massachusetts
1790–1810
Mahogany with birch

The seat rails are birch. All four corner blocks are missing, and the right arm has been repaired at the rear where it joins the back.

H. 43½″　　w. 25¾″　　D. 22″
(110.49 cm.)　　(65.43 cm.)　　(55.88 cm.)

PROV.　John S. Walton, Inc., New York.

This type of tall, upholstered chair with open arms and tapering legs was widely made in New England toward the end of the eighteenth century and is commonly known today as a "Martha Washington" chair. Charles Montgomery has speculated that the term "lolling chair," frequently found in inventories of the period, probably refers to this sort of chair, although in Virginia, at least, the term appears as early as 1755,[1] certainly predating this particular form. The only embellishment on this chair is the molded contour of the front of the legs and arm supports, which tapers off onto the arm itself.

1971-364

1. Inventory of the estate of Dr. Kenneth McKenzie taken August 18, 1755. York County, Wills and Inventories, no. 20 (1745–59), pp. 364–66.

BRUSH-EVERARD HOUSE, Northwest Bedroom

DRESSING TABLE, *Massachusetts,*
1730–60. (No. 145).

UPHOLSTERED ARMCHAIR,
Massachusetts or New Hampshire,
1800–1815. (No. 64).

64

64 UPHOLSTERED ARMCHAIR
Northeastern Massachusetts or southeastern
    New Hampshire
1800–1815
Mahogany with maple and lightwood inlay

The seat rails are maple, the inlaid panels above the front legs are probably birch. There is no indication of corner blocks. The sides of the chair have been upholstered at one time, and tack holes are visible on both the interior and exterior of the arms.

H. 45½″   W. 25″   D. 22″
  (115.57 cm.)   (63.50 cm.)   (55.88 cm.)

PROV. John S. Walton, Inc., New York.

PUBL. *Antiques* 97 (June 1970), p. 5.

Several related Sheraton-style chairs of this form are known to exist, but few approach this example in design and execution. The graceful serpentine of the cresting rail is emphasized by the S curves of the arms and arm supports and a small quarter-round block has been glued behind the top of the arm support to ease the visual transition between the arm and its support. The legs taper gracefully and terminate in high peg feet, further accentuating the verticality of the chair. Inlay of the type used on the face of the arm supports, composed of husks with black and white dots, is generally credited to Massachusetts, and particularly to the Salem area. A gentleman's secretary at Winterthur is labeled by Edmund Johnson and embellished with similar inlay.[1] A Portsmouth, New Hampshire, attribution has been made for at least one chair in this group,[2] based primarily on the figured rectangular panel above the legs, a feature found on a number of pieces of Portsmouth furniture.[3] Other examples of the form are illustrated in Sack, *Fine Points,* page 73, and in the Cornelius C. Moore sale catalog.[4]

1971-421

1. Montgomery, No. 179.
2. Charles E. Buckley, "Fine Federal Furniture Attributed to Portsmouth," *Antiques* 84 (February 1963), p. 200, fig. 9.
3. Ibid., pp. 196–200.
4. *Important American Furniture . . . From the Estate of the Late Cornelius C. Moore* (New York: Parke-Bernet Galleries, October 30, 1971), Lot 92.

65

66

65 UPHOLSTERED ARMCHAIR
Probably Massachusetts
1790–1810
Mahogany with maple and oak

The framing of the back is mahogany, the seat and arms are maple, and the bracing strips beneath the arms are white oak. Both front legs are pieced below the stretchers, all corner blocks have been replaced, and the tenons of the seat rails are mortised through the rear legs behind the upholstery of the back.

H. 43″   w. 27¾″   D. 23¼″
  (109.22 cm.)   (70.51 cm.)   (59.03 cm.)

PROV. John S. Walton, Inc., New York.

This highly individual chair is a cross between an easy chair and an upholstered armchair of the type of the two preceding examples. In place of the normal exposed wooden arms, this chair has been fitted with stuffed, horizontally rolled arms in the manner of an easy chair. The only comparable example known is a chair at Winterthur of similar design in which the arms are rolled vertically.[1] The significance of the through tenons in the construction of the seat rails has not as yet been determined, but if indeed the above attribution is correct, it is the only instance yet known where this feature was used in Massachusetts.

1971-365

---

1. Montgomery, No. 122.

66 EASY CHAIR
Probably Masachusetts
1750–90
Walnut with maple, white pine, and chestnut

The front legs and stretchers are walnut, the rear legs and frame, except the arms, are maple. The arms are made in two pieces glued together vertically: the outer half of each arm is white pine, the inner half of one is maple, the other, chestnut. The chair is entirely original with the exception of two small repairs where the stiles join the cresting rail; the many tack holes indicate the chair has been upholstered several times, and several eighteenth-century nails remain in the frame. The rear legs are made in one continuous piece with the stiles.

H. 46½″   w. 35⅞″   D. 21⅜″
  (118.11 cm.)   (91.12 cm.)   (54.29 cm.)

PROV. L. G. Myers, New York.

PUBL. *Girl Scouts,* No. 567.

This is the classic New England easy chair, in completely original condition. One marvels that such sparing use of wood in the frame is sufficient to prevent the chair from collapsing from use, but there is no evidence of stress or repair. The shape of the leg and foot is very close to that on side chairs Nos. 53 and 54.

1930-121

67

68

67 EASY CHAIR
Probably Massachusetts
1750–90
Walnut with maple

All legs and stretchers are walnut and the seat rails are maple. Corner blocks have been added, but the chair does not appear to have had any originally.

H. 46″ W. 32⅛″ D. 23⅛″
  (116.84 cm.) (81.60 cm.) (58.71 cm.)

PROV. Luke Vincent Lockwood; Parke-Bernet Galleries, New York.

PUBL. *XVII and XVIII Century American Furniture and Paintings: The Celebrated Collection Formed by the Late Mr. and Mrs. Luke Vincent Lockwood,* (New York: Parke-Bernet Galleries, May 13, 14, and 15, 1954), Lot 317; Lockwood II, fig. 508 (this appears to be the same chair).

This chair differs from No. 66 principally in the flatter front foot and in the chamfering of the rear legs above the stretchers. The rear legs are spliced to the stiles at an angle rather than forming one continuous piece as in the previous chair. Both methods were used in New England in the eighteenth century, but when the back legs were made in one continuous piece, maple stained to resemble the primary wood was generally used as it was less expensive.

1954-349

68 EASY CHAIR
Probably Newport, Rhode Island
1750–90
Walnut, cherry, maple, and white pine

The front legs, and the side and medial stretchers are black walnut; the rear legs, back stiles, and lower back brace are cherry; the seat rails are maple; the remainder of the frame is white pine. There is no evidence of corner blocks ever having been attached to the seat frame. All four knee brackets are replacements, as is the rear stretcher; both front feet are cracked and have been repaired; casters were once attached to the feet.

H. 47⅝″ W. 28½″ D. 21¾″
  (120.96 cm.) (72.39 cm.) (55.24 cm.)

PROV. The Earl B. Osborns, Northampton, Mass.

Although this chair is of the conventional New England type, it is smaller and lower than the average example and is exceedingly interesting from a constructional point of view. The combination of walnut and cherry as primary woods is very unusual, maple being much more common for the back legs. Characteristic of Newport workmanship are the low proportions, the rounded seat, the lack of corner blocks, and the rear legs and stiles made of continuous pieces of wood (this method was also practiced elsewhere in New England, but lasted longer in Newport). Most interesting is the unusual manner in which the front legs are attached to the seat rails. Most New England chairs are fastened at the corner with a simple mortise-and-tenon joint, the rails mortised into the leg which extends upward, forming the corner of the seat. In this example, however, the two rails are lapped over in the Philadelphia manner, but instead of the leg being dovetailed into the rails as was usual in Philadelphia, here the top of the leg comes up through the center of the rails in a quarter round. The inner edges are flattened aft, while the front edge follows the curved outline of the rails. This type of lapped joint can be seen on another Newport chair, but its leg does not protrude through the rails.[1] This chair is the only example known of this unusual but practical method of construction.

For another, documented, Newport chair of similar design, differing principally in having square corners, see *Antiques,* December 1971, frontispiece. Owned by the Metropolitan Museum of Art, the chair is covered with its original needlework and is signed and dated by Gardner of Newport, 1758, on the crest rail.

1967-626

---

1. Morrison H. Heckscher, "Form and Frame: New Thoughts on the American Easy Chair," *Antiques* 100 (December 1971), p. 888, fig. 6.

69

69 EASY CHAIR
Probably Newport, Rhode Island
1765–90
Mahogany with maple

The primary wood is mahogany; the frame is maple and white pine. Replaced corner blocks of tulip have been added as reinforcements beneath the frame. The medial stretcher is probably a replacement, and there are several cracks and gouges on the legs and stretchers.

H. 46″   W. 29⅝″   D. 22¼″
   (116.84 cm.)   (75.25 cm.)   (56.49 cm.)

PROV. L. G. Myers, New York.

Stop-fluted easy chairs are among the rarest forms in American furniture. A virtually identical example was exhibited at the Metropolitan Museum of Art in New York in 1963.[1] A second example was included in the John Brown House loan exhibition in Providence in 1965.[2] It has horizontally scrolled arms in the Philadelphia manner rather than the conventional New England cone type as on the other two chairs. A third example, still retaining its original linen undercovering and webbing, was owned by Israel Sack, Inc., in 1973.[3]

1930-410

----

1. James Biddle, *American Art from American Collections,* (New York: Metropolitan Museum, 1963), p. 40. This chair can also been seen stripped of its later upholstery in *Sack Brochure 1* (January 1957), No. 24.

2. *John Brown Catalog,* No. 26. This chair is illustrated stripped in Morrison H. Heckscher, "Form and Frame: New Thoughts on the American Easy Chair," *Antiques* 100 (December 1971), p. 889.

3. *Sack Brochure 23,* No. P3684.

70

71

70 CHEST WITH DRAWER

Probably Connecticut
1700–1730
White pine with yellow pine and oak

The body of the chest is white pine, the feet are oak, and the rear board of the base is yellow pine. The front of the chest is divided by single arched moldings to simulate three drawers, the upper two of which are false. The left side molding is missing. The single drawer has two wood pulls; there is no evidence to suggest pulls were ever attached to the upper false drawers. The top is hinged with staples at the rear. The sides of the drawer are nailed at the front and rear. The sides of the chest are lapped over the front and back boards. The red paint which covers the exterior appears to be original. The feet are doweled into the base, and there is no center board beneath the drawer.

H. 28¼″	w. 37½″	D. 17⅛″
(71.76 cm.)	(95.25 cm.)	(43.50 cm.)

PROV. Lillian Blankley Cogan, Farmington, Conn.

Chests of this type must have been very common in New England during the first third of the eighteenth century, but few examples have survived. A chest of very similar design with higher ball feet was owned by Mrs. Richard T. Fisher of Petersham, Massachusetts, in 1929.[1] Yellow or "hard" pine is often found in Connecticut pieces of the seventeenth and early eighteenth centuries.

1955-265

---

1. Russell H. Kettell, *The Pine Furniture of New England* (Garden City, N.Y.: Doubleday, Doran & Co., 1929), No. 35.

71 CHEST WITH DRAWERS

Maker: Possibly Jonathan Small
Massachusetts, possibly Harwich
1720–50 (with later additions)
White pine with yellow pine, maple, and oak

This chest has a hinged lid which opens to reveal an interior half the depth of the case. The two top courses of drawer fronts are false. The case is of white pine with maple molding strips, except for the strip above the top drawer, which is of pine; the drawer linings are partly of white pine and partly of yellow pine; the backboards are yellow pine; the two bottom boards and the interior blocks of the feet are oak. The bracket feet are old (with the exception of the right rear and some repairs to the others), but are not original to the chest. The green paint is mostly old and has been touched up in places, and there are remnants of white wriggle-work decoration on both sides over the green. The drawer sides have been built up, and the right front molding is a replacement, as is the lower half of the left molding strip. The wire hinges to the top are original. The two backboards are nailed on and the drawer sides are nailed at all four corners. The escutcheon of the center top is original; all other brasses are old copies.

H. 39″	w. 36⅜″	D. 17⅞″
(99.06 cm.)	(92.40 cm.)	(45.43 cm.)

PROV. According to a paper found in the drawer, the chest was made by Jonathan Small of South Harwich, Massachusetts.

This chest has been rather extensively restored and would not normally be included in a catalog of this sort. It is interesting, however, to see the way in which an early chest can be "modernized" to try to bring it up to date. Originally, the sides extended behind the base molding to the floor and were cut out to form the feet. Subsequently, probably late in the eighteenth century or early in the nineteenth, the sides were cut off slightly above the molding and the present bracket feet were added. According to a family genealogy, there were two Jonathan Smalls in Harwich, Massachusetts, who could have made this chest.[1] Jonathan Small, Sr. (ca. 1683–ca. 1778), was the son of Edward of Falmouth, Maine, and later Chatham, Massachusetts. Jonathan married, at Harwich, Damaris Winslow in 1713 and had a son Jonathan, born in 1721. No occupation was listed for either Jonathan Small, but Edward, the father of Jonathan, Sr., was a carpenter who superintended the building of the church in Chatham in 1700. While there is no proof of the attribution of this chest to either Jonathan Small, the style of the piece is consistent with other chests known to have been made in southeastern Massachusetts during the period, particularly some of the larger chests made at Taunton.[2] The white wriggle-work decoration, presently visible only on the sides under a strong light, probably originally decorated the entire surface of the chest.

Anonymous gift

G1971-576

_____

1. Lora A. W. Underhill, *Descendants of Edward Small of New England* (Boston: Houghton Mifflin, 1934).

2. Esther Stevens Fraser, "The Tantalizing Chests of Taunton," *Antiques* 23 (April 1933), pp. 135–38.

72 CHEST WITH DRAWER
Massachusetts, Taunton area
1725–50
White pine

The chest is made entirely of white pine; the original hinges to the lid are missing, and the lid is presently fastened to the chest with a pair of iron butt hinges of later date. There are several long splits in the front above the drawer, and the drawer pull is probably a replacement. A piece is broken off the outside edge of the left front foot. Some paint has been lost, particularly on the top, but there is no evidence of either the red ground or the white decoration having been repainted.

H. 21″	w. 22⅜″	D. 13″
(53.34 cm.)	(57.46 cm.)	(33.02 cm.)

PROV. Miss Mary Allis, Fairfield, Conn.

According to Esther Stevens Fraser, whose article contains virtually all of the published information about the small group of chests like this one, a characteristic example has three distinctive elements of design: a tree or vine springing

from a wavy line, the use of C curves in place of leaf forms, and the use of a cluster of dots at the end of the Cs.[1] The small chest here illustrated contains all of these elements, but differs from other examples in that the artist has delineated leaves on the branches of the front of the chest above the drawers. This chest is very similar to an example then owned by Mrs. Fraser and illustrated in her article (fig. 3) and also to a more elaborately painted example initialed *HB* at the Art Institute of Chicago.[2]

AARFAC F.71.1

_____

1. Esther Stevens Fraser, "The Tantalizing Chests of Taunton," *Antiques* 23 (April 1933), pp. 135–38.

2. Comstock, No. 180.

73 CHEST
Probably Connecticut
1825–40
Tulip, white pine, and cherry

The four sides and feet are tulip, the top and bottom are white pine, the till is cherry. There is an old split in the left rear corner of the top, and the right rear corner of the base has been repaired. The sides are dovetailed to the front and back. The lock, hinges, and feet are original, as is the red paint.

Each iron butt hinge is stamped *T Clark*.

H. 18″	w. 25½″	D. 13⅝″
(45.72 cm.)	(64.77 cm.)	(34.61 cm.)

This small, simple, and late chest is included here principally because of its original condition and the marked hinges. "T. Clark" is as yet unidentified.

Anonymous gift

G1971-524

72

73

74

75

74 CHEST OF DRAWERS
Massachusetts
1760–90
Mahogany with white pine

All brasses are original; the bottom of the escutcheon on the top drawer has been cut off to allow it to fit the drawer. Each drawer is framed with a single bead except at top and bottom. The side talons of the well-formed feet rake to the rear; the rear and inside edges of the back feet are unfinished and squared off. The drawer sides have been built up, and the drawer runners are early replacements. The lock in the bottom drawer has been removed and the space filled in with mahogany. The third drawer has a small repair in the lower left corner.

H. 32⅛″   w. 35¾″   D. 21″
   (81.60 cm.)   (90.80 cm.)   (53.34 cm.)

PROV. Israel Sack, Inc., New York.

PUBL. *Sack Brochure 20,* No. P3326.

A black-and-white photograph does not do this chest sufficient justice, for one does not see the superb color or appreciate the magnificence of the compact proportions. Few comparable examples exist in any collection, public or private.

1972-228

75 CHEST OF DRAWERS
Probably Massachusetts
1770–1800
Mahogany with white pine

All secondary wood is white pine. The top and both sides are each composed of two separate boards. The brasses and some drawer runners are replacements.

H. 32⅛″   w. 36⅛″   D. 20⅜″
   (81.57 cm.)   (91.76 cm.)   (51.76 cm.)

It is interesting to compare this chest with No. 74, for while both have serpentine fronts, there is little other similarity between them. The serpentine is reversed here from the preceding chest and is blocked at either end rather than flowing in a continuous line to the side mouldings. The top follows the same profile, as do the enormous feet with their deeply scrolled brackets. It seems obvious that this chest was a much less expensive piece of furniture and that it was probably not made in an urban center such as Boston. An allied chest with very closely related feet descended in the family of Zadoc Lincoln of Hingham, Massachusetts.[1]

Gift of the estate of Mrs. Ernest J. Hanford
G1965-112

---

1. *Sack Brochure 17,* No. 1228.

76

77

76 HIGH CHEST OF DRAWERS
Probably Massachusetts
1760–1800
White pine

This chest is made entirely of white pine. The scroll of the left front foot bracket is missing. The brasses are original.

H. 53½″   W. 38½″   D. 19″
(135.89 cm.)   (97.79 cm.)   (48.26 cm.)

A simple chest, distinguished only by the scrolled brackets flanking the high feet, this example is unusual in the use of pine as the primary wood.

Anonymous gift
G1965-4

77 CHEST OF DRAWERS
Eastern Massachusetts or southern New
    Hampshire
1800–1820
Cherry with mahogany, birch, white pine,
    light and dark wood inlay

The primary wood is cherry; the drawer fronts are mahogany veneer on white pine surrounded by borders of figured birch; the drawers, backboards, base, and all interior framing are white pine; the inlaid escutcheons and light wood stringing appear to be maple; the dark inlaid border of the top appears to be rosewood. The drawer knobs are replacements, and markings on the drawer fronts indicate that the chest was originally equipped with circular brass backplates and bails. The interior drawer runners are replaced, and the drawer sides have been built up. The right front column has been screwed through the top and plugged, the locks in the top three drawers are missing, and there is some insect damage in the back.

H. 39½″   W. 48⅝″   D. 21-1/16″
(100.33 cm.)   (123.51 cm.)   (53.50 cm.)

This chest is a classic document of the manner in which the rural cabinetmaker adapted a sophisticated urban design and changed the details and materials to reflect his or his client's tastes and/or means. The inspiration of the design of this chest is a rather large group of Boston furniture made between 1810 and 1820. Representative of these pieces are three chests of drawers with mirrors attached: two at Winterthur[1] and one at the Museum of Fine Arts in Boston.[2] One of these examples is labeled by Levi Ruggles, but there were probably several Boston (and possibly Salem) cabinetmakers involved in their production.

The Boston chests are constructed primarily of mahogany with mahogany, birch, and maple veneers. The front posts vary in design but are reeded, and the legs taper to pad or small ball feet. One example has ivory-bound keyhole escutcheons.

The Williamsburg chest is similar to the Boston pieces in design but differs consistently in details and construction. The primary wood is cherry rather than mahogany. The front columns are fluted, but appear clumsy because of their long drop from top to skirt without a break. The fluted drums below the reeded columns are similar to those on the two Winterthur chests but are longer and coarser in execution. The feet are seemingly original inventions of the maker. The lock escutcheons, very similar in design to those used by John Seymour on a number of pieces,[3] are here made of light wood rather than the ivory favored by the Boston makers.

The exact area of production of this chest is difficult to determine, although it was obviously in the Boston sphere of influence. A labeled mahogany example by Samuel Noyes of Sudbury, Massachusetts (to the west of Boston), once owned by Benjamin Flayderman,[4] is similar but differs in details. Another bow-front example, this one made of cherry, bears the label of John Gould, Jr., of New Ipswich, New Hampshire.[5]

Anonymous gift
G1971-540.

---

1. Montgomery, Nos. 144, 145.
2. Randall, No. 37.
3. Montgomery, No. 185.
4. *American Furniture* (New York: American Art Association, Anderson Galleries, Inc., April 17, 18, 1931), Lot 130.
5. *New Hampshire Arts,* No. 70.

78

*Reuben Box 1084 / Nellie Box 14 /   Box   /
Hiram Box 387.* In crayon on other side of
drawer: *Hiram Keeler.* In pencil on second
drawer from right in third row of upper section:
Grandpa Judson's Medicine Chest. Roman numerals
scratched into drawer bottoms.

H. 64⅞″   W. 40¾″   D. 14¼″
   (164.81 cm.)   (103.53 cm.)   (36.20 cm.)

PROV. According to information accom-
panying the chest, this piece was made in the
second half of the eighteenth century by Dr.
Reuben Warner of Bridgewater, Litchfield
County, Connecticut. Dr. Warner supposedly
made the piece for his son, Dr. Reuben Warner
II (1782–1828). The chest then passed to his
daughter Emily and was used by her husband,
Dr. Horace Judson. The piece remained in the
family until 1948. J. K. Byard, Norwalk, Conn.

Although there is no specific reason to doubt
the history of this chest as given above, it seems
unlikely that the piece was made by an ama-
teur. The chest is very finely made and was most
likely the production of a well-trained craftsman. Apothecary chests of this type were relatively common in Connecticut and other areas
of rural New England, but seldom are they
found in a full Queen Anne style.

1950-635

78 CHEST ON FRAME
Connecticut, probably Litchfield area
1760–1800
Cherry with tulip and white pine

All framing and drawer linings are tulip except
for the drawer runners and the rear of each
drawer, which are white pine. The front of the
lower right drawer in the upper section has been
repaired as has the cornice molding on the right
rear of the upper section. Several brass knobs
have been replaced. The drawer sides are
molded on the top and the drawer bottoms are
nailed at the rear with a single rose-headed nail.
The back of the case is fastened to the sides and
top with large wooden pegs.

Pencil inscriptions on second drawer from
right in fourth row of upper section: *L   Box /*

79 HIGH CHEST OF DRAWERS
Probably Connecticut
1750–1800
Cherry, white pine, and oak

All secondary wood is white pine with the exception of white oak braces beneath the bonnet.
The drops are missing and the brasses replaced,
the lips of several drawers are patched, and the
drawer runners are replacements.

Several inscriptions on top of lower section:
By Steamer _____ / to Albany. Peter Bunn and *Peter Bun* written several times. *Ostrander* on paper
label on rear of upper section, *C. P. Sanders /
Schenectady / By Rail [Road] / from Albany.*

H. 91½″   W. 41″   D. 21¾″
   (232.41 cm.)   (104.14 cm.)   (55.24 cm.)

79

PROV. This chest descended in the Sanders family of Scotia, New York. The earliest definite mention of the piece in any of the family papers is in an inventory taken between 1900 and 1923 of the effects of Charles P. Sanders II (1856–1923). Its ownership by his father, Charles P. Sanders I (1824–1891), is indicated by the label on the back of the chest. Charles P. Sanders I, who married Jane Livingston Ten Broeck in 1846, was the son of Peter Sanders (1792–1850) and his wife Maria (Elmendorf), the daughter of Peter Edmund Elmendorf and Elizabeth van Rensselaer. Peter Sanders's father was John Sanders II (1757–1834), whose wife was Albertina Ten Broeck. With this rather complicated background of well-known New York names, it is impossible to confirm the original owner of this chest or to ascertain how it came into the family. Robert Palmiter Antiques, Bouckville, New York.

PUBL. John M. Graham II, "Scotia Furnishings," *Antiques* 89 (January 1966), p. 100; *The Glen-Sanders Collection from Scotia, New York* (Williamsburg, Va.: Colonial Williamsburg, 1966), No. 17.

This chest has previously been published as New York, based on its long history in that state. While it is conceivable that a chest of this type could have been made in the Albany-Schenectady area, no bonnet-top, high chest of drawers with a firm New York history is known, and a comparison of this piece with documented Connecticut examples makes an attribution to that area much more probable. A virtually identical Connecticut example, smaller in size and with different finials, is known.[1]

The significance of the inscription on the lower section of the chest has not yet been determined. The chest obviously came to Albany by steamer (sometime in the early nineteenth century, judging by the writing). The logical place for it to have come from would be New York City, and several members of the family are known to have had furniture shipped up the river from New York. The name "Bunn" is found in the New York directories of the early nineteenth century, but the first name "Peter" has not yet been discovered. A New York City attribution is unlikely, however, because of the use of cherry and the distinct provincial character of the piece. Other items of New England furniture (notably the so-called Boston chairs) found their way to Albany; probably this chest too was made in Connecticut, shipped to New York City, and then up the Hudson to Albany.

1964-246

---

1. *Sack Brochure 16*, No. 1143.

80

80 HIGH CHEST OF DRAWERS
Boston, Massachusetts
1740–60
Maple with white pine frame

This piece was repaired and restored in the 1950s. Some repainting, regilding, and repair of gesso was done, and the finials and drops were made at that time. Locks are missing from the second and fourth long drawers in the upper section. The drawer dividers are lap-jointed into the sides in the upper section, while those in the lower case are dovetailed. There is a full dust board beneath the top row of drawers in the upper section and beneath the bottom drawer, half dust boards between the other drawers. The japanning is done on a black ground.

ᘯ appears on the back of almost every drawer. The word *back* is written on the back side of four drawers. The drawers are numbered on the back with a combination of arabic and roman numerals. *Command* is written across the back of the right drawer in the lower case. Several drawers have figuring and various initials, including *JP* in script on the inside of one of the small drawers in the lower section.

H. 84½″   w. 43⅞″   D. 23½″
   (214.63 cm.)   (111.47 cm.)   (59.69 cm.)

PROV. The chest was exhibited at the Metropolitan Museum in 1933 when it was owned by Miss Margaret Danforth of Boston. The previous history is unknown. John S. Walton, Inc., New York.

In examining this chest and its relationship to other examples, one must consider separately the design of the piece itself and the decoration. This writer knows of five bonnet-top, japanned, high chests in addition to the Williamsburg example: the so-called John Pimm example at Winterthur,[1] the Pickman example at the Metropolitan Museum,[2] the Brewster family example at Bayou Bend,[3] a chest at the Colonel Josiah Quincy House in Wollaston, Massachusetts, and an unrestored and much-defaced example currently on loan to the New Haven Colony Historical Society. In addition, at least two flat-topped examples seem related to the group: a recently restored chest at the Baltimore Museum of Art[4] and one in the Bolles Collection

at the Metropolitan Museum. All of the bonnet-top examples are basically similar in design; all are constructed of maple and pine; each has a scrolled, open bonnet; and all originally had three finials. The drawer arrangement is similar, although there are variations in size; all have similar front skirts composed of three flat-headed arches; all have plain cabriole legs, each ending in a pad foot with the exception of the Winterthur example, which terminates in an unusual claw foot.

While the similarities in design are close, the Williamsburg piece differs from the other examples in several respects. First, the profile is quite broad. The width of almost 44 inches contrasts with approximately 41 inches for the other examples. The cabriole legs are high and straight, although they are close in profile to the New Haven and Quincy examples. The lower portion of the chest is shallow, again like the New Haven example, and the drawers, particularly the lower row at the base and the center drawer at the top, are less vertical than on any of the other chests. The shells on the drawer of the Williamsburg chest are not carved as those on the Pickman, Winterthur, and Bayou Bend examples, but merely built up with gesso. This feature is found also on the Quincy and Bolles chests and was probably done in this manner on the New Haven piece. The most obvious difference is the use of gilded, fluted pilasters in the upper section, a feature that does not appear on any of the other examples. In this feature, the piece is much closer to a number of undecorated Boston high chests and chests-on-chests.[5]

That one japanner was responsible for the decoration on all of these chests is unlikely. The Bayou Bend and the Metropolitan examples are quite similar in design. The decoration is heavily done and consists mainly of groups of figures and architectural features. The carved shells are flanked by painted pilasters, and winged cherubs' heads decorate the spandrels.

The decoration on the Williamsburg chest is related in various ways to that on the Winterthur, Baltimore, and Quincy chests. On all four of these pieces, the design consists primarily of animals, birds, and flowers. The same small one-masted boats that appear on the lower drawers of the Williamsburg chest also appear on the Winterthur and Baltimore examples. The reclining lion on the left side of the lower drawer in the upper section is identical to one found on the Quincy chest. All four pieces lack the columns flanking the shells, and the spandrels are filled with gilt floral bouquets and geometric designs rather than cherub heads. Similar brasses are found on all examples. An unusual feature of the Williamsburg piece, which does not occur on any of the other examples, is the large circular medallion above the top center drawer in the upper section.

In short, any positive attribution of this piece is difficult to make. In form it is closely allied to the New Haven and Quincy chests, but the presence of the applied pilasters separates it from all the other examples. The decoration is most closely related to that on the Winterthur and Quincy examples, and all three may have been done by the same man. The initials *JP* on the inside drawer might lend some credence to designating John Pimm the decorator, but one must also consider Robert Davis whose signature appears on the Baltimore chest. Perhaps the word *Command,* as yet not understood, will eventually provide a further clue.

1959-100

1. Fales, No. 99.
2. *The American Heritage History of Colonial Antiques* (New York: American Heritage, 1967), fig. 194.
3. *Collectors and Collections* (New York: *Antiques* Magazine, 1961), p. 22.
4. *Antiques* 103 (July 1973), p. 1070.
5. Lockwood i, No. 95; Randall, No. 54.

81 CHEST-ON-CHEST

Massachusetts, Boston or North Shore
1770–90
Mahogany with white pine

All secondary wood is white pine; several drawer runners are replacements. There are several minor cracks in and repairs to the case. The brasses and finials are original. The drawer sides follow the outline of the case and are double-beaded on the top edge.

1896 painted on top of base, *315½* scratched near it, paper pasted beneath pediment on left side on which is visible *T/ L* and *2 doz/50408.*

AB in red crayon on left side of top left drawer.
H. 91¾″   W. 46″   D. 23⅞″
(233.07 cm.)   (116.84 cm.)   (60.64 cm.)

PROV. Francis G. Shaw, Wayland, Mass.

PUBL. *Antiques* 63 (March 1953), p. 232.

Bombé furniture is rare, and perhaps the rarest form of all is the chest-on-chest, or double chest. Only three other examples are known to this writer: a virtually matching piece owned by the Museum of Art, Carnegie Institute;[1] a chest owned in an Ipswich, Massachusetts, family in 1933, obviously related to the Williamsburg and Carnegie examples but lacking the carved rosettes and differing in other details;[2] and the great masterpiece made and signed by John Cogswell in 1782.[3]

It is an accepted fact among furniture historians that all American bombé furniture was made in Boston. The only fully documented pieces—the Cogswell chest mentioned above and the George Bright desk at the Boston Museum[4]—are both by Boston makers, and other examples are known with good Boston histories. While undoubtedly much, if not most, bombé furniture was made in Boston itself, it seems likely that cabinetmakers in surrounding areas also made furniture in this style. In comparing the three related pieces exemplified by the Williamsburg chest with several documented North Shore, Massachusetts, and particularly Marblehead chests, one can see a number of similarities in design.

At the Detroit Institute of Arts is a chest-on-chest with a blocked lower section on claw-and-ball feet.[5] The upper section of the chest is similar in almost every detail to the Williamsburg bombé example. The chest is signed *NB 1774* and is attributed to Nathan Bowen of Marblehead. A closely related double chest at the Museum of Fine Arts in Boston has a serpentine lower case, but again a very similar upper section.[6] This piece is signed by Bowen and Ebenezer Martin, also of Marblehead, and is dated 1780. A third chest, at the Essex Institute in Salem, is tentatively attributed to Bowen and Martin on the basis of a faint chalk inscription.[7] A number of other related chests with North Shore histories also exist. A comparison of the

81

Williamsburg, Carnegie, and Nutting examples (the latter, interestingly enough, attributed in 1929 to an Ipswich cabinetmaker) with the Marblehead chests reveals a number of close similarities. All have similarly designed upper sections, each with four large drawers below three smaller drawers, the smaller of which are shaped to follow the profile of the cornice, and the central drawer carved with a fan. In the Williamsburg and Carnegie examples the top inner corner of the outer drawers comes to a false point. In the other examples this area is flattened out. The drawers in all the chests are framed with a bead on the case, and the drawer sides have a double arch on top. The drawers of all examples are flanked with fluted Doric pilasters, similar in design except for the minor differences in the molding at the top. The design of the cornice, central plinth, and finials is essentially the same in all examples. The Boston Museum piece and that at the Essex Institute lack the carved rosettes. It is impossible at this point to say specifically that this chest was made in Marblehead or elsewhere on the North Shore. Perhaps the several inscriptions, about which no conclusion has yet been reached, will provide a clue. Nevertheless, the similarities between the bombé chests and the documented Marblehead examples is too close to ignore, and the possibility definitely exists that at least some bombé furniture was made in the Essex County area.

1935-343

1. *American Art from American Collections* (New York: Metropolitan Museum, 1963), No. 57.

2. Nutting, *Treasury III,* p. 277.

3. *Antiques* 61 (April 1952), pp. 322–24.

4. Randall, No. 64.

5. Richard H. Randall, Jr., "An Eighteenth-Century Partnership," *Art Quarterly* 23 (Summer 1960), p. 152.

6. Randall, No. 41.

7. Fales, *Essex County Furniture,* No. 75.

82 HIGH CHEST OF DRAWERS
Maker: Attributed to a member or members of the Booth family
Connecticut, Southbury area
1780–1800
Cherry with oak, tulip, and white pine

The primary wood is cherry; all drawer sides are oak; the drawer bottoms, some drawer backs, the drawer runners, dustboards, backboards, bottom of upper section, and bonnet are tulip; the remainder of the drawer backs are white pine. The chest is in almost entirely original condition. The tip of the right front cornice of the upper section has been repaired, two lower backboards of the upper section have been renailed, and small pieces of both scrolls on the center finial have been broken. The brasses are original, the finish is old. There is some evidence that the upper and lower sections were made by different craftsmen. The oak in the drawer sides of the lower section is of a different cut than that in the upper section, and the dovetails on the drawers are narrower in the upper section. The drawer runners in the upper section are nailed from the top; in the lower section, they are nailed from the sides into the case itself (see also below).

H. 90" (228.60 cm.)　w. 44" (111.76 cm.)　D. 22¾" (57.78 cm.)

PROV. According to family tradition, this chest was made by Elijah Booth of Southbury, Connecticut, as a wedding present for his daughter. It descended in the Stiles family of Southbury until recent times. Kenneth Hammitt, Woodbury, Conn.; David Pottinger, Bloomfield Hills, Mich.

A number of related desks and high chests of drawers have been discovered in the Southbury and Woodbury areas of Litchfield County, Connecticut. Most of these have been attributed to Elijah Booth (1745–1823), his brother Ebenezer, or Ebenezer's son Joel. Although no labeled or completely documented examples are known, most pieces have descended in local families with strong oral attributions to members of the Booth family. The family cabinetmaking business has been well documented by Ethel Hall Bjerkoe.[1] Ebenezer, the oldest brother, died in

1789 and left a considerable estate consisting of joiner's tools, chair parts, chests and desks, and a large amount of cherry, oak, whitewood (tulip poplar), pine, birch, and maple. Elijah's inventory revealed no tools and few pieces of furniture, but many years before his death he had sold his joiner's shop to Eli Hall. Joel Booth, the oldest son of Ebenezer, died suddenly in 1794, and his estate included a joiner's shop and several partly completed pieces of furniture in the shop, including chests of drawers, desks, tables, clock cases, and other forms. In addition, he left a large quantity of mahogany, cherry, whitewood, and pine boards.

As all three of these family members were working at approximately the same time, it is impossible to separate their work without further documentation. There are a number of individual features, however, which tie the various pieces together. Closest in form to the Williamsburg chest is a similar example formerly owned by John J. Gunther.[2] Part of the bonnet of that piece has been repaired, but the similarities are obvious. Particularly significant are the short, rounded cabriole legs with beaded edges and grasping claw feet. A desk and bookcase owned by Professor and Mrs. James W. Marvin has been attributed to Elijah Booth for many years.[3] It has the same deep shell in the lower case and

82

82a

the same short, beaded legs, this time terminating in unusual Spanish feet. At Winterthur is a related desk and bookcase with similar shell and feet and chamfered, fluted corners topped by rosettes similar to those on the Williamsburg chest.[4]

As indicated above, the upper and lower sections may possibly have been made by different hands. The two pieces are well integrated, however, and the brasses on both sections are the same and original. The most likely conclusion would seem to be that one part of the chest was made by one member of the family (perhaps Ebenezer or Joel), left unfinished at his death, and later completed by another member.

1972-413

1. Ethel Hall Bjerkoe, "The Booth Family of Newtown and Southbury, Connecticut," *Old-Time New England* 68 (Summer 1957), pp. 8–11.

2. *New England, Philadelphia & New York Cabinetwork* (New York: Parke-Bernet Galleries, Inc., October 21, 1960), Lot 252.

3. *Litchfield County Furniture, 1730–1850* (Litchfield, Conn.: Litchfield Historical Society, 1969), No. 40.

4. Downs, No. 231.

83 TALL-CASE CLOCK

Maker: William Claggett
Newport, Rhode Island
1745–65
Mahogany with chestnut, white pine, and
  aspen

The backboard of the case, the back of the hood, the seat block, and the base are chestnut; the interior blocking is of white pine and aspen (the aspen blocks may not be original, but have been part of the case for some time). The finials are old (with the exception of the left plinth block) but are not original to the clock. The brass fret has had some minor repairs but is essentially original; the small circular areas at either side probably originally had brass inserts. Evidence of old red wool was found behind the brass fret over the sound holes, and old wool of similar color has been installed in this area. Several brass rods have been replaced in the columns flanking the hood. The brass capitals at the top and bottom of the rear hood columns were missing and new ones have been made copying those on the front columns. The shell on the door to the trunk and the panel on the base had shrunk from the case and have been refitted. All four feet had been cut approximately one inch below the base; they have been restored, copying those on a closely related case. The works and pendulum are in their original working condition. Remnants of the original silvering were visible on the dials, and they have been resilvered.

Rectangular name plate in center of dial: *Will Claggett / Newport.*

H. 100¼"	W. 21⅜"	D. 11⅝"
(254.64 cm.)	(54.29 cm.)	(29.52 cm.)

PROV. By tradition, this clock was taken to New Brunswick during the Revolution by a Loyalist and remained there until shortly before its acquisition by Colonial Williamsburg. Mr. Harry B. Carleton, East Providence, R.I.

There is little question that this clock is one of William Claggett's finest productions. The dial is not as elaborate as that on the japanned-case example once owned by William Ames of Providence[1] or that owned by Samuel G. Babcock.[2] But in its simpler (and possibly earlier) design, it is a superb example. It differs only in minor details from one owned by G. Winthrop Brown[3]

83a

and one in the collection of the Henry Ford Museum.[4] All three of these clocks have an arched dial plate with a secondary dial in the arch, which is used to determine the time of high tide in a given area. Dials of this form are known on English clocks, but this writer knows of no other examples by an American maker. A circular opening in the dial displays the phases of the moon. In two of the examples the maker's name is on a rectangular plate in the lower center of the main dial. In the Brown example, it is on an arched plate in the same area.

The cases of Claggett's clocks vary in design as much as the dials and show a distinct progression in style from the earliest examples with domed hoods and ball feet[5] to the arched hood and block-and-shell-carved door of the Williamsburg clock, undoubtedly the latest case housing Claggett works known. If proof could be found that the case was made at the same time as the works, this clock would be one of the key documents of Newport furniture, for that would necessarily date it before 1750 (Claggett died in 1749) and would establish the use of the blocked shell in Newport much earlier than had previously been thought. However, there are several indications that the case was made perhaps twenty to thirty years after the works.

A study of various Claggett clocks indicates that the works in this example were made by Claggett sometime in the middle of his career, probably before 1740. The comparison of the various dials would seem to confirm this, as the dial on this clock is probably earlier than the elaborate moon dials on the Ames and Babcock clocks previously discussed. The style of the case, a popular one in Newport for at least twenty years, also seems later than 1749. A very similar case houses works by Seril Dodge, who was working in Newport from 1760 to 1785.[6] Another example, at the Rhode Island Historical Society, is fitted with English works made by Marmaduke Storrs, working in London from 1760 to 1774. A key example is the labeled case by John Townsend at the Metropolitan Museum of Art.[7] Numbers on the label have been interpreted as 1769, which, if correct, would confirm the dating of these other examples. The closest example of all would seem to be a clock whose works were made by William Creak of London, working 1740 to 1768.[8]

While the case of this clock does seem related to these other examples, it retains a number of earlier features. The magnificent pierced brass fret may be unique on a Newport clock (a similar fret of paper appears on a clock at Winterthur made by James Wady of Newport about 1750;[9] Wady was Claggett's son-in-law). Fretwork of this type also appears on at least one Boston-made clock, a japanned-case example made by Gawen Brown in 1766 and owned by the Henry Ford Museum.[10] The use of brass rods as stop flutes on the hood columns would appear to be earlier than the use of the more common wood flutes.

Most important, the form of the blocked shell on the door would seem to be a very early example. The lobes are simply formed with little detail, and the center portion was left empty rather than carved as on most examples. In this respect, it is similar to the two James Wady clocks, the one at Winterthur previously cited and another,[11] both of which probably date before 1760. The conclusion to be drawn from all this evidence is that while the works of this clock probably predate the case by at least twenty years, the case is a very early example of its type. Probably made about 1760, it is most likely one of the earliest-known examples of the Newport block front.

1972-36

1. Lockwood II, figs. 842–43.
2. "William Claggett of Newport, Rhode Island, Clockmaker," *Old-Time New England* 27 (January 1937), p. 115.
3. Nutting, *Treasury II,* No. 3249.
4. Comstock, No. 18.
5. Randall, No. 200.
6. *John Brown Catalog,* No. 78.
7. Nutting, *Treasury II,* No. 3265.
8. *Sack Brochure 19,* No. P3293.
9. Downs, No. 202.
10. Comstock, No. 187.
11. *John Brown Catalog,* No. 76.

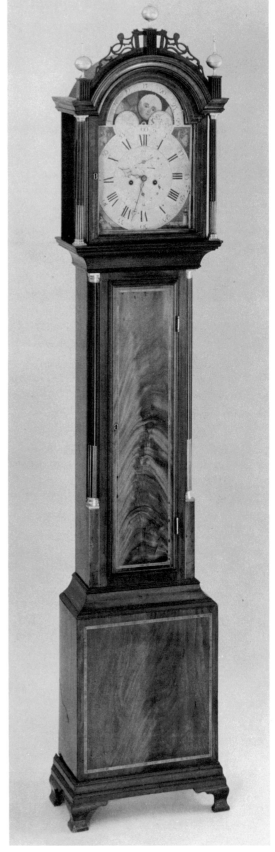

84 TALL-CASE CLOCK

Maker: Aaron Willard
Boston, Massachusetts
1800–1810
*Mahogany and mahogany veneer with white
pine*

All secondary wood is white pine. The left front
foot has been repaired at the base, and several
of the interior bracing blocks have been
replaced.

Dial signed *Aaron Willard*. Label of Willard
inside case, pencilled repair inscriptions on door
of trunk:... *7–23–97 / Dec 12, 1877 / L. B.
Coombs, March 18, 84 / James Adams December 21,
1859.*

H. 100⅛″	W. 21″	D. 10″
(254.32 cm.)	(53.34 cm.)	(25.40 cm.)

PROV. Israel Sack, Inc.; Anderson Galleries,
New York.

PUBL. *Important Colonial Furniture and Decorations—Property of Israel Sack, Boston, Massachusetts*
(New York: American Art Association, Anderson Galleries, Inc., November 7, 8, and 9, 1929),
No. 376.

This clock is one of the finest productions of
Aaron Willard's manufactory known to this
writer. The painted dial is ambitious and well
conceived; the wood for the case was carefully
selected and matched. The heavy molded base
with ogee bracket feet is unusual on Aaron Willard clocks, the lighter French foot being more
common, and this feature may indicate a relatively early date. A comparable clock with
French feet was made for Joshua Seaver in
1806.[1]

1930-52

---

1. *Sack Brochure, 14,* No. 855.

85

85 BANJO CLOCK

Maker: Aaron Willard, Jr.
Boston, Massachusetts
1815–30
Mahogany with white pine

Some of the blocks inside the case have been replaced, green wool cloth has been glued to the
case behind the works, and the eagle finial is a
replacement. The works includes a striking
movement.

A. Willard, Jr. / Boston painted on dial; *Patent*
in scroll on waist glass, *436495* scratched into
back of dial, *499* stamped into rear of waist

panel, *500* stamped inside back and on top rear of bottom door.

H. 42⅜"	W. 10⅜"	D. 4½"
(107.64 cm.)	(26.36 cm.)	(11.43 cm.)

PROV. Israel Sack, Inc., New York.

John Ware Willard stated in his authoritative work that Aaron Willard, Jr., did not sign his name to clocks until his father's death in 1823.[1] However, several of Willard's so-called banjo clocks, including this example, are so close in style to those produced by Simon Willard in the first decade of the nineteenth century that it seems likely that Aaron Jr. was signing his name to dials several years earlier than 1823. A similar clock, with the same painted chariot scene on the bottom door, was owned by Israel Sack, Inc., in 1964.[2]

1971-376

1. John Ware Willard, *A History of Simon Willard, Inventor and Clockmaker* (Boston: n.p., 1911).
2. *Sack Brochure 12,* No. 704.

86 DAYBED
Massachusetts or Rhode Island
1720–40
Maple

The wood portions of this bed have been damaged by insects, in some areas rather extensively. The second foot from the head on the left side is a replacement, a narrow iron rod apparently once extended through all the center stretchers from front to back, and two cross braces beneath the seat are missing. The black paint is cracked and chipped; it appears to be original. The leather covering has been patched, but at least part of it seems to be original.

H. 40⅜"	L. 67½"	W. 21¾"
(102.56 cm.)	(171.45 cm.)	(55.24 cm.)

PROV. Acquired in Rhode Island by David Stockwell, Inc., Wilmington, Del.

The broad, horned-yoke crest, the rectangular, upholstered back, and the delicately vase-turned legs seem to be unique features of this magnificent daybed. No similar example has been found, which is surprising considering the successful combination of the various elements. The provenance of the piece is difficult to determine, as most of the individual features were used in several areas of New England. Lending some support to a Rhode Island attribution, where the piece was found, is the existence of a cabriole-leg side chair with a similar crest and back.[1] The same crest rail, however, is also seen on a number of New Hampshire chairs[2] and on several North Shore, Massachusetts, examples credited to the Gaines family.[3] See also two chairs in this catalog, Nos. 41 and 43.

1954-379

1. *John Brown Catalog,* No. 1.
2. *New Hampshire Arts,* No. 14.
3. *Sack Brochure 20,* No. P3315.

86

86a

87

87 DAYBED

Massachusetts or Rhode Island
1730–70
Maple

The bed is made entirely of maple, including the original corner blocks behind the front legs. The corner blocks beneath the head legs have been replaced, as have the knee bracket of the left head leg and the longitudinal stretcher nearest the head. The crest rail has been repaired and reattached, and both head legs are split near the base. The webbing is not original, and the piece has been stained a dark brown all over.

H. 38⅜″   L. 62⅞″   W. 22″
  (97.48 cm.)   (159.73 cm.)   (55.88 cm.)

PROV. John S. Walton, Inc., New York.

Queen Anne–style daybeds of this type are generally called Rhode Island, principally, it seems, on the basis of an example sold at auction in New York in 1932, supposedly made in 1743 by Job Townsend for the Eddy family.

That example is currently in the Metropolitan Museum.[1] Similar although not identical examples are at Winterthur[2] and the Museum of Fine Arts in Boston,[3] and several other examples are known.[4] All vary in specific features, probably indicating manufacture over a wider geographical area than Rhode Island. The profile of the cabriole legs, the turning of the stretchers, and the blocking and chamfering of the rear legs relate this example to the Winterthur bed; however, it lacks the scalloped skirt, and the back is fixed rather than adjustable. It is the only example seen on which the ears scroll to the rear rather than to the sides.

1957-56

1. *Antiques* 50 (October 1946), p. 251.
2. Downs, No. 212.
3. Randall, No. 190.
4. *John Brown Catalog*, No. 87; Lockwood II, Nos. 644, 645.

88 SOFA

Massachusetts, Salem area
1805–15
Mahogany with bird's-eye maple veneer and
  white pine

All secondary wood examined is white pine.
H. 36½″   w. 60″   D. 22″
  (92.71 cm.)   (152.40 cm.)   (55.88 cm.)

PROV. Israel Sack, Inc., New York.

PUBL. *Sack Brochure 18,* No. 1409.

The design of this small sofa is taken from plate 35 of Thomas Sheraton's *The Cabinetmaker and Upholsterer's Drawing Book* (London: n.p., 1793). In place of the carved baskets of fruit and swags found on many Salem examples of this general type, the craftsman who made this example has veneered the crest panels with bird's-eye maple.

1971-380

89 SOFA

Massachusetts, Salem area
1805–20
Mahogany and mahogany veneer with maple
  and white pine

The front skirt is veneered on white pine, the remainder of the visible frame is maple. The back and arms have not been examined.
H. 34¼″   w. 68¼″   D. 22″
  (86.97 cm.)   (173.36 cm.)   (55.88 cm.)

PROV. John S. Walton, Inc., New York.

No other sofa of this exact form has been seen, but the various elements are related to known Salem-area pieces. The craftsman has simplified the basic Sheraton design but followed the instructions for a square sofa in the *London Chair-Makers' and Carvers' Book of Prices for Workmanship, 1802* (No. 3, pl. 11, p. 83), where it is described as "Framing with turn'd stumps and front legs in one piece, an upright behind ditto, and elbows sweep'd towards the top." The legs of this sofa are closely related to those on a small sideboard at the Museum of Fine Arts in Boston, made by William Hook of Salem in 1808/9.[1]

1971-367

1. Randall, No. 70.

88

89

90

91

90 DRESSER
New England
1760–1820
White pine

Part of the red paint seems to be original, but it has been touched up at least once in several places; there has been some scraping and water damage around the feet. The shelves have been nailed through the backboards in recent times and were not originally attached in that manner, a wood catch was once affixed to the door, and part of the door escutcheon is missing.

H. 71⅜″   W. 43″   D. 19″
  (181.92 cm.)   (109.22 cm.)   (48.26 cm.)

PROV. Israel Sack, Inc., New York.

It is very difficult to assign a date to a piece such as this, as the form was unquestionably made over a long period. The hardware is probably eighteenth-century in date, but it seems possible that the escutcheon, at least, was taken from an earlier piece.

1952-320

91 HANGING CUPBOARD
Probably Connecticut
1740–1800
White pine throughout

The cupboard is made entirely of white pine and retains its original red paint. With the exception of minor chips and rubs, it is in its original condition. The inside is fitted with a pair of shelves.

There are several lines of penciled inscriptions inside the door, most of which are illegible. Visible are the names *Bull* and *Hill* and the dates *1905* and *1911*. It may possibly be a record of birth. The letter *N* and figure *8* or letter *B* are scratched into the door.

H. 30″   W. 26⅜″   D. 8¾″
  (76.20 cm.)   (67 cm.)   (22.25 cm.)

PROV. Lillian Blankley Cogan, Farmington, Conn.

1955-264

92

92a

92 CUPBOARD-DESK
Probably Massachusetts
1760–1800
White pine with maple

This piece is made in two sections. The carcass and framing are white pine, the front of the slide and the slide supports are maple. The hinges and lower escutcheon are original, the upper escutcheon is a replacement, both locks are replacements, and there is a large patch inside the right door of the lower section where the original lock was located. The backboard has been reattached. The interior of both sections has been stained a dark red; the original green-painted exterior was revealed after the removal of several later coats.

In ink on bottom of slide: *For Mr. Arthur Little / Repaired by / W. A. Macomber / #2 Byron Street Boston / Mass / December 15, 1892.*

H. 82″   W. 47½″   D. 13½″
(208.28 cm.)   (120.65 cm.)   (34.29 cm.)

PROV. John S. Walton, Inc., New York.

PUBL. Fales, *Painted Furniture,* No. 116; *Antiques* 68 (September 1955), p. 190.

The architectural influence on this piece is obvious: the intricate moldings, the fluted pilasters, the fielded panels. Not so evident is the skillful manner in which these elements are combined to lighten and define this basically awkward form. The pilasters are three flutes wide on the lower section, only two on the upper. The height of the upper section has been visually reduced by the use of small fielded panels at the top instead of extending the larger panels all the way up. The starkness and repetitiveness of the interior of the upper section has been broken by facing the dividers with a simple scallop border. The original use of the piece is unknown, but it probably served as an office desk rather than as an apothecary or kitchen cupboard.

1955-235

93

93 BOOKCASE

Probably Massachusetts
1810–20
Mahogany, white pine, and maple

The upper part of this bookcase is made of five individual sections (cornice, center bookcase, two wings, and backboard), all of which are screwed together. The lower part is unitary. The exposed top of the lower section is solid mahogany, the cornice and the front of the base molding are of mahogany veneered on white pine, the door fronts are mahogany veneered on maple, the sides of the carcass and base molding are white pine stained to resemble mahogany; all other secondary wood is white pine. Several panes of glass have been replaced. All elements of the upper section are held together with modern screws, but original screw holes are visible. The interior of the upper section was painted green at one time. Curtains were once hung inside the glazed doors and the center door of the upper section once had a plate escutcheon. The pulls to the doors in the lower section are replacements, as are some interior shelf supports.

J or *G* painted in script on backboard; *June 12, 1792* in pencil on upper inside rail of left center door of lower section.

| H. 87¼″ | w. 62″ | D. 17⅛″ |
| (221.62 cm.) | (157.48 cm.) | (43.50 cm.) |

PROV. Israel Sack, Inc., New York.

PUBL. *Sack Brochure 18,* No. 1478.

The most interesting feature of this bookcase is the sparing use of mahogany in its construction; only the absolute minimum was used. Whether this reflects the decision of a client who wished to keep the price down or of a cabinetmaker whose supply of the wood was limited is difficult to determine. Because of this feature, the provenance of the piece is also open to speculation. A similar piece with a secretary drawer in the lower section descended in the Van Rensselaer-Crosby family of New York and has been assigned to that city.[1] The large amount of white pine used in the construction of this piece, however, would seem to indicate a New England origin, and the sophistication of style points toward the Boston area. The 1792 date is undoubtedly spurious.

1971-375

---

1. *Sack Brochure 2,* No. 96.

94

95

94 STAND-UP DESK

Massachusetts, probably North Shore
1700–1750
White pine throughout

Made as a unit, the desk was originally painted or stained red, but is now covered with a light blue-gray paint which may itself be of eighteenth-century date. The sliding shelf is a later addition but probably dates from the early nineteenth century. The cross supports on which the shelf sits are nailed to each leg, a section of which has been rabbeted out to receive them. The slides on which the shelf rests when pulled forward are recent replacements, but a fragment of one original slide is stored with the desk. All joints are fastened by nails or pegs; the only dovetails secure the drawer front to the sides. The interior is plain and unpainted, with two small drawers below a row of pigeonholes. All brasses and escutcheons are original, as are the large butterfly hinges securing the lid to the top.

In ink inside well of desk: *J. Gyles Merrill's Harvard College 1755.* In a different hand, *James C. Merrill's Desk / Harvard College / October 6, 1803.* Inside lid are scratched a number of later inscriptions copying those above; *S M* carved on original slide runner.

H. 51¼″   w. 32¼″   D. 19¼″
   (130.18 cm.)   (81.92 cm.)   (48.90 cm.)

PROV. This desk is one of the best-documented pieces of New England furniture in the Colonial Williamsburg collection. It was continuously owned in the Merrill family from at least 1755 until the middle of this century. Gyles Merrill was born in Salisbury, Massachusetts, in 1738/9, a fourth-generation descendant of the immigrant Nathaniel, who settled in nearby Newbury in 1635. He graduated from Harvard in 1759 and received his A.M. in 1762. In 1765 he was ordained pastor of the North Church in Haverhill and served until his death in 1801. In 1767 he married Lucy Cushing, daughter of Reverend James Cushing. Their son James Cushing Merrill was born in Haverhill in 1784, graduated from Harvard in 1807, and received his A.M. in 1810. He resided in Boston, practiced as a lawyer, and represented Boston in both branches of the state legislature. Israel Sack, Inc., New York.

PUBL. *Harvard Tercentenary Exhibition: Catalogue of Furniture, Silver, Pewter, Glass, Ceramics, Paintings, Prints...* (Cambridge: Harvard University Press, 1936), No. 249, pl. 44; Thomas Hamilton Ormsbee, "Bible Boxes were Also Desks," *American Collector* 11 (November 1942), p. 6, pl. 3.

The desk would seem to be considerably earlier in date than its first recorded use in 1755. The elongated double-baluster and ring turnings are found on New England furniture dating as early as the latter part of the seventeenth century. No exactly comparable desk has been found, although a number of two-piece desks-and-frames from this period are known.

1952-629

95 DESK

Probably Massachusetts
1765–1800
Mahogany with white pine

The hinges to the lid have been replaced, there is a small repair to the center of the left slide, the lock is missing from the third long drawer, the bottom drawer was never fitted with a lock, and all brasses are original.

There are chalk numbers on the back of each drawer.

H. 42¼″   w. 42¼″   D. 21⅝″
   (107.32 cm.)   (107.32 cm.)   (54.92 cm.)

PROV. L. G. Myers, New York.

The simplicity of the exterior of this desk is counterbalanced by the finely blocked and shell-carved interior. The talons on the well-formed ball-and-claw feet do not rake backward as in most Massachusetts examples, but extend straight downward.

1930-36

96

97

96 DESK

Probably Connecticut
1765–95
Birch with maple, tulip, white pine, and
basswood

The carcass of the desk is birch, the feet and brackets are maple, the interior drawers have birch sides and tulip backs and bottoms, the case drawers have basswood sides and white pine bottoms and backs, and the back and bottom framing of the desk are tulip and white pine. The desk has been scraped and refinished. A strip has been inserted across the center of the lid and is probably a replacement, all exterior brasses are replacements as are the hinges to the lid, one small interior drawer has new sides, the drawer runners are replaced, and the drawer sides have been built up.

JE in script written on base.

H. 42½″   w. 35½″   D. 20¾″
(107.95 cm.)   (90.17 cm.)   (52.70 cm.)

The unusual combination of woods in this piece makes attribution difficult. Basswood *(Tilia)*, also known as linden, was, according to one authority (Montgomery), principally used in New Hampshire and northeastern Massachusetts, but two tables at Winterthur attributed to Rhode Island are partially made with this rarely used wood. Tulip is not normally found in furniture made north of Connecticut and Rhode Island. The flattened claw-and-ball feet seem most related to Connecticut workmanship and can be compared with a desk in the Barbour Collection at the Connecticut Historical Society[1] and another desk, at the Litchfield Historical Society, which also has the rear feet squared off in the same manner.[2]

Gift of Mr. and Mrs. Roger W. Peck.
G1969-215

---

1. *Frederick K. and Margaret R. Barbour's Furniture Collection* (Hartford: Connecticut Historical Society, 1963), pp. 62–63.

2. *Litchfield County Furniture* (Litchfield, Conn.: Litchfield Historical Society, 1969), No. 38.

97 DESK

Massachusetts
1765–95
Mahogany with white pine

All brasses are old but not original except those on the side of the case. The hinges to the lid have been replaced and the area surrounding the hinges has been patched. The drawer sides are crudely chamfered on both inside and outside edges.

Chalk numbers are on the rear of full-length drawers.

H. 44¼″   w. 45″   D. 22½″
(112.40 cm.)   (114.30 cm.)   (57.15 cm.)

This desk is a typical, well-made Massachusetts example, similar in overall style to a large number of related pieces. The extreme simplicity of the interior, broken only by the pilastered document drawers, probably indicates the particular desires of the client rather than lack of skill by the maker.

Anonymous gift
G1971-538

98

98a

98 DESK

Maker: Attributed to Benjamin Frothingham
Massachusetts, Boston or Charlestown
1765–1800
Mahogany with white pine

The interior of the desk is entirely white pine. The two document drawers flanking the central door of the interior are false and do not open. There are cracks on the interior of the lid around all three hinges; the center crack extends through the lid and is visible when the lid is closed. All drawer sides in the lower section have been built up. A split down the left side has been tightened with butterflies from the inside; a split in the base molding at the left of center has been repaired with a screw. There was apparently once a center drop on the skirt, which has disappeared, although the supporting block is visible. All brasses are original, with the exception of the lid escutcheon.

H. 42″   W. 44½″   D. 24″
(106.68 cm.)   (113.03 cm.)   (60.96 cm.)

PROV. Israel Sack, Inc., New York.

PUBL. *Antiques* 63 (March 1953), p. 234; Alice Winchester, ed., *Antiques Treasury* (New York: E. P. Dutton & Co., 1959), p. 76.

This desk has been attributed to Rhode Island since its acquisition by Colonial Williamsburg, but a careful study of the various elements would seem to indicate Boston or Charlestown as its most likely source. The shells and lunette drawers of the interior are closely related to the George Bright secretary at the Museum of Fine Arts, Boston,[1] and the interior arrangement is very similar to the hairy-paw Massachusetts desk in the Karolik Collection at the Museum of Fine Arts.[2] The closest parallels of all are found in the documented works of Benjamin Frothingham of Charlestown. A labeled secretary owned in 1952 by William Earls has a very similar interior,[3] as does a labeled desk with claw-and-ball feet at Deerfield.[4] A number of Frothingham's labeled pieces have virtually identical exterior blocking, including the Deefield desk, a chest of drawers owned in 1952 by Mrs. Ernest L. Rueter,[5] and a chest-on-chest owned by John P. Kinsey.[6] On none of the documented Frothingham desks are the lids blocked as in this example, but several attributed pieces do have this feature, including a fine hairy-paw secretary.[7] Of particular importance to the Frothingham attribution are the similarities between the front feet of the Williamsburg desk and those on the Kinsey chest.

1930-210

1. Randall, No. 64.
2. Hipkiss, No. 25 and Supplement photo 25.
3. Mabel Munson Swan, "Major Benjamin Frothingham, Cabinetmaker," *Antiques* 62 (November 1952), p. 392.
4. Samuel Chamberlain and Henry Flynt, *Historic Deerfield* (New York: Hastings House, 1965), p. 170.
5. Swan, op. cit., p. 395.
6. Ibid., frontis.
7. Helen Comstock, "Frothingham and the Question of Attributions," *Antiques* 63 (June 1953), p. 505.

99

100

99 DESK

Probably Rhode Island or southeastern
  Massachusetts
1760–90
Mahogany with white pine and chestnut

All secondary framing is white pine with the exception of a portion of the foot blocking, which is chestnut. All brasses are original with the exception of the pulls to the slides and some interior pulls. The left rear foot blocks have been screwed to the bracket; the right rear foot blocks are missing. The backboards have been off and reattached, but appear to be original.

Chalked numbers on back of large drawer; scratched roman numerals inside each drawer front.

| H. 42″ | w. 41½″ | D. 21″ |
| (106.68 cm.) | (105.41 cm.) | (53.34 cm.) |

PROV. L. G. Myers, New York.

Although in general form this desk is similar to a number of Newport examples, it is rather crudely constructed and lacks the fine detailing one would expect in Newport craftsmanship. The interior shells are similar to Boston workmanship, and, in fact, the interior of the desk is quite similar to the attributed Frothingham desk (No. 98). However, the shaping of the feet and the presence of chestnut as a secondary wood seem to indicate Newport influence. The rather awkward and unattractive manner in which the center door is hinged appears on other Newport desks, including a labeled blockfront example by John Townsend[1] and a large secretary in the Karolik Collection at the Museum of Fine Arts in Boston[2] which descended in the Cooke family of Rhode Island.

1930-206

------

1. *Sack Brochure 21,* No. P3448.
2. Hipkiss, No. 20.

100 DESK

Maker: Attributed to Stone and Alexander
Boston, Massachusetts
1790–1800
Mahogany with light and dark wood
  inlays and white pine framing

The hinges to the lid and several of the small interior brass pulls are replacements; all other brasses are original. The right drawer in the upper level of the interior is a modern replacement. The lip of the top has been repaired around the lock, the lock in the top full-length drawer is missing, and the other locks are replacements. All drawers in the case have been lined with blue paper. The central interior door is secured only by a lock at the top and a brass pin at the bottom. When unlocked, the door comes off completely, revealing two drawers and a pigeonhole behind.

Penciled inside front of lower center drawer of interior: *Repaired and finished by L. R. Fuller / Shelburne Falls Mass. June 10, 1901.* Shipping tag found in drawer: *H. S. Swan Company / Dealers in / Furniture / Shelburne Falls, Massachusetts.*

| H. 45″ | w. 46″ | D. 24½″ |
| (114.30 cm.) | (116.84 cm.) | (62.23 cm.) |

PROV. According to a written history compiled in 1916 by its owner, this desk was originally the property of a family named Grant who lived on Pinckney Street in Boston on or before 1800. The Grants gave the desk as a wedding present to Mr. and Mrs. Cotton Strong of Boston, who subsequently moved to Mt. Holly, Vermont, and then to Chester, Vermont. The desk then passed to their daughter Sarah (Strong) Crowly Wright, wife of Deacon Samuel Wright of New Salem, Massachusetts, who sold it for $75 in 1901 to Mrs. F. E. Fairbanks of Shelburne Falls, Massachusetts, who had it polished by H. S. Swan Co. in that year. The desk remained in the family and was owned by Mrs. Fairbanks's great-grandson, Francis C. Hadley, in 1955. There seems little doubt that the family for whom the desk was made was that of Moses Grant, the prosperous Boston upholsterer and paper manufacturer who was a participant in the Boston Tea Party in 1773. Although, far as can be determined, he never lived on Pinckney Street (which was not laid out until 1802), he did live nearby on Cambridge Street. It is also known that Cotton Strong worked as a paperhanger in Boston in the 1820s, almost certainly for the firm then being run by descendants of Moses Grant. Good and Hutchinson, Tolland, Mass.

This desk is identical in virtually every respect to an example labeled by the Boston cabinetmakers Stone and Alexander, who are listed in the Boston directory of 1796 as working together.[1] The only notable variations are a slight difference in the shaping of the knee bracket and the fact that the labeled desk has side handles. Significantly, the inlaid door on the labeled example, while slightly different in execution, lets down in the same manner as this one and is the only other door of this type found. The writer also knows of a labeled serpentine chest of drawers by the same firm with identical feet and knee brackets.

The firm of Stone and Alexander was in business from about 1792 until 1796 at Prince and Back streets. In addition to the labeled desk mentioned above, there is a single side chair at Winterthur bearing a different label[2] and a pair of chairs with labels dated 1792 at the Henry Ford Museum.

1970-100

1. Sack, *Fine Points,* No. 147; *American Collector* 6 (September 1937), p. 11.
2. Montgomery, No. 31.

101 SECRETARY
New England
1770–1800
Cherry with white pine

The sides and backs of all drawers are chamfered slightly on the outside edges. The bottoms of the small drawers are nailed and glued to the sides; the bottoms of the large drawers in the lower section are slotted in and nailed at the back. The interior document drawers are false. The backboards in both upper and lower sections are composed of three vertical boards, feather-edged and finely made. All brasses are old, but not original. The frets above two of the pigeonholes and the hinges to the lid have been replaced. The finial blocks are supported by iron braces at the rear.

Chalk numbers on rear of interior drawers. *A . . . .* Benjamin[?] scratched into the top drawer of the lower section.

H. 85″   w. 43½″   D. 22½″
(215.90 cm.)   (110.49 cm.)   (57.15 cm.)

It is difficult to know where to assign the manufacture of this delicate and finely crafted piece. In some ways, notably the treatment of the bonnet and the blocked interior, it reminds one of Rhode Island or eastern Connecticut workmanship. In other areas, such as the fine serpentine curve of the base and the shaping of the ogee panels of the top, one thinks of Boston or North Shore, Massachusetts, workmanship. However, the use of cherry and certain idiosyncrasies in design and construction make a tentative attribution to western Massachusetts or Connecticut more probable.

The desk interior is similar, although not exactly so, to several published Connecticut examples. The profile of the foot is related to that on a chest of drawers from New London County[1] and similar softly twisted corkscrew finials are seen on several Connecticut case pieces. No parallel has been found for the center finial, nor for the unusual but practical scrolls nailed to the front of the slides.

A careful study of this well-designed and superbly proportioned small secretary will reward the viewer with a new appreciation of eighteenth-century craftsmanship at its best.

Anonymous gift
G1971-542

1. Kirk, *Connecticut Furniture,* No. 58.

101

101a

102

103

102 SECRETARY

Massachusetts or New Hampshire
1760–90
Mahogany with white pine

One inch has been added to the base of all four feet, and the interior drawer runners have been replaced. The rear brackets of the rear feet are replacements, as is the corner block inside the right rear foot; baize or leather had once been attached to the inside of the desk on the lid.

H. 60⅞″   w. 41½″   D. 20¼″
  (154.62 cm.)   (105.41 cm.)   (51.44 cm.)

PROV. L. G. Myers, New York. Apparently acquired by him in Virginia.

Desks and chests with a small, delicate, pendant shell beneath the center of the skirt are generally attributed to Salem, principally, it seems, on the basis of a serpentine chest with canted corners labeled by William King of Salem and formerly in the collection of Mrs. J. Insley Blair.[1] It seems likely, however, that this detail was not confined to Salem, but was utilized throughout much of Massachusetts and probably in New Hampshire as well. Only one other example of a desk with a similar small bookcase top is known to this writer.[2] It has a serpentine desk section supported by bracket feet, and no history is attached to it. Another inlaid example with the same serpentine molded panels on the bookcase section can be seen in a charming interior view of the farm house of Moses Morse of Loudon, New Hampshire, painted in 1824 by Joseph Warren.[3] According to Mrs. Nina Fletcher Little, the owner of the painting, Morse is said to have been a cabinetmaker, but his name is not listed in published sources.

1930-145

1. *Antiques* 12 (September 1927), frontis.
2. *Antiques* 101 (March 1972), p. 485.
3. *New Hampshire Arts,* No. 104.

103 SECRETARY

Probably New Hampshire
1780–1800
Mahogany with white pine, maple, and
light and dark wood inlay

The hidden top of the lower section is maple; all other secondary wood is white pine. There is a small repair at the center top of the cornice. The escutcheons on the upper doors are original, all other exterior brasses are replacements. The locks are missing from the second and fourth drawers of the lower section. The interior of the upper section has a row of pigeonholes across the top faced with ogee brackets similar in shape to those in the lower section. Below the pigeonholes the bookcase interior is divided vertically by a fixed partition with two adjustable shelves on each side. The rear feet of the lower section are cut off square at the back and on the inside.

H. 87½″   w. 44⅞″   D. 23⅞″
  (222.25 cm.)   (113.98 cm.)   (60.64 cm.)

PROV. Winick & Sherman, New York.

This secretary is very similar in design to a birch and mahogany example in the Currier Gallery of Art in Manchester, New Hampshire, said to have been made by Enoch Poor of that city.[1] While the Currier piece has a scrolled bonnet and lacks the inlaid cornice and slides, in all other details it is practically identical: the shaping of the ogee panels in the bookcase section, the arrangement of the desk interior, the serpentine of the lower section, and the sharp knee and shaping of the ball-and-claw feet.

1930-128

1. *New Hampshire Arts,* No. 50.

104

105

104 SECRETARY

Massachusetts, probably Boston
1805–15
Mahogany with mahogany and curly maple veneer and white pine

The oval patera on the face of the pediment, the tympanums between the arches of the doors, and the elongated bases beneath each column are veneered with curly maple. The fronts of the drawers in the lower section are veneered on white pine. The interior of the upper section is composed of two shelves made of white pine and faced with mahogany. The upper shelf is adjustable. Below the lower shelf is a row of seven pigeonholes with arched brackets at top, below which are three small drawers, the right-hand one fitted with compartments. The slant lid folds forward and rests on two slides to form a writing surface. All finials, brasses, the drawer runners in the lower section, and the side brackets flanking the legs are replacements; the front brackets are original. Gilt has flaked off three of the four panels in the door.

Gum sticker on rear of right finial block: M._____ / 39617 / Mrs. Lovell [?].

H. 74¼″   W. 37½″   D. 21½″
(188.60 cm.)   (95.25 cm.)   (54.61 cm.)

PROV. Israel Sack, Inc., New York.

PUBL. *Sack Brochure 19,* P3236.

It is tempting to attribute this piece to the workshop of John and Thomas Seymour, but close comparison with the documented Seymour examples shows little justification for such an attribution. There is little of the distinctive inlay and exciting contrasts of color found on labeled Seymour examples, the drawer escutcheons are brass rather than ivory, and the brackets and other carved details lack the meticulous crispness for which the Seymours are known. As Richard Randall has so brilliantly pointed out in a pair of articles, many other Boston cabinetmakers working in the early years of the nineteenth century utilized the same designs and the same subsidiary craftsmen as did the Seymours;[1] thus it is extremely difficult to attribute any of this work to a specific craftsman without identifying documentation.

Although no secretary exactly comparable to this example has been discovered, two somewhat related pieces have been published. A secretary owned by the Rhode Island School of Design has a very similar upper section with virtually identical eglomisé panels, although it includes a pair of drawers below the blind panels.[2] The lower section is also similar in design, although the shaping of the legs is quite different. Eleanor Bradford Monahan attributes that secretary to Providence,[3] but lacking additional examples of similar Rhode Island work, this writer feels a Boston attribution is safer.

A third secretary which was shown in the Girl Scout loan exhibition has a similar upper section but lacks the eglomisé panels. The legs are also quite close in design, although they appear shorter and heavier than in this example.[4]

Similar reeded legs with elongated, rounded feet are found on a card table and chamber table at Winterthur;[5] both pieces are attributed to Boston. While both are tentatively assigned to the Seymour shop, Montgomery acknowledges that other Boston cabinetmakers were capable of similar workmanship.

1971-374

_____

1. *Antiques* 81 (February 1962), pp. 186–89; and (April 1962), pp. 412–15.
2. Stoneman Supplement, No. 16.
3. *Antiques* 87 (May 1965), p. 578.
4. *Girl Scouts,* No. 691; also illustrated in Stoneman, No. 51.
5. Montgomery, Nos. 307, 338.

105 SECRETARY

Northeast Massachusetts or New Hampshire
1800–1810
Mahogany and mahogany veneer with white pine

All secondary wood is white pine. The fall front is veneered on mahogany and the prospect door in the interior and the four drawers in the lower section are veneered on white pine. Several small pieces of veneer and molding are missing, the brasses are replacements, the escutcheons are missing from the lid and prospect door; the blocking beneath the feet is intact and original. There are large cracks in both sides of the lower section. There is no evidence of finials ever having been attached to the piece.

Alexander Johnson / Fayetteville, North Carolina scratched on left side of top drawer behind prospect door in upper section; *TWB* in pencil on base of second long drawer in lower section; *T [or S] WB* in pencil on base of third long drawer; *Bottom* in script on base of bottom drawer.

H. 87½″   w. 38″   D. 19¾″
  (222.25 cm.)   (96.52 cm.)   (50.17 cm.)

PROV. Mrs. B. L. Brockwell, Petersburg, Va.

PUBL. *Antiques* 63 (March 1953), p. 237.

Secretaries of this general type were made in an area from Boston northward to Portsmouth, New Hampshire. This example, while well made, is unusual in that the writing lid folds down from the upper section rather than outward from the top of the lower section as it does in most examples. This arrangement not only makes for awkward proportions of the entire piece, but the lid itself is supported only by the ledge of the lower section and slants forward so that nothing can rest on it when opened. Only one other example of this arrangement has been seen.[1] The inscription in the upper section and the fact that this piece was acquired in Virginia probably indicates that this secretary is another example of New England furniture exported to the South at the time of its manufacture.

1930-151

---

1. Nutting, *Treasury I,* No. 736.

106 DESK ON STAND
Maker: Lewis Bigelow
Paxton, Massachusetts
1800–1807
White pine

The desk is presently covered with a coat of dark red paint which seems to have been the

original color of the upper section, but beneath the red on the lower section a light blue-green paint is visible and seems to have been the first color. The lock inside the drop lid is missing; the hasp and staples presently securing the lid when closed were probably added after the lock was removed but have been in place for some time. The original brass pulls of the slides are missing and crude nails have been substituted.

In pencil on left inside drawer bottom: *Property of Lewis Keith whose / mother was formerly / Persis Bigelow—married Francis Keith / The Bigelow Desk / made by Lewis Bigelow.* In pencil on bottom of right inside drawer: *Bigelow Desk.* In ink on top of front of right inside drawer: *$12 $10 60.* In pencil on bottom of large drawer: *1926 / owner Lewis Keith Hoar / Grandson of Lewis Keith of Barre, Vt. / Bigelow Desk.*

H. 41¾″   w. 22¾″   D. 16″
  (106.05 cm.)   (57.78 cm.)   (40.64 cm.)

PROV. The desk was apparently made by Lewis Bigelow (1780–1807) of Paxton, Massachusetts, son of Ithamer and Persis (Barrett) Bigelow of that town. Lewis died unmarried and the desk descended from his niece, Persis Bigelow (1798–1838), daughter of Timonthy and Anna (Earle) Bigelow of Paxton, Massachusettts, and Barre, Vermont. Persis Bigelow married Francis Keith of Barre and they had a son Lewis. From him the desk descended to his grandson, Lewis Keith Hoar, also of Barre, who, according to the inscription on the lower drawer, owned the piece as late as 1926.

Seldom is it possible to state with any accuracy the date and provenance of a simple piece of country furniture such as this charming small desk. The fortunate preservation of the penciled jottings inside the drawers, combined with genealogical sleuthing, has made it possible not only to identify a previously unknown craftsman of the central Massachusetts area but also, because of his short life, to narrow the probable date of production to a limited time span. One wishes other families had been as careful in chronicling their furniture.

Anonymous gift
G1971-553.

106

106a

107

108

109

107 LOOKING GLASS
New England
1730–70
White pine

The top of the crest has been repaired, and the glass is probably an early replacement; the frame is painted black, and the decorative flowers and leaves are painted in red and yellow. Much of the decoration on the frame has been worn away.

H. 13⅜″   W. 6¾″
(34.61 cm.)   (17.15 cm.)

PROV. Lillian Cogan, Farmington, Conn.

PUBL. Fales, *Painted Furniture,* No. 102.

1964-468

108 LOOKING GLASS
New England
1740–70
White pine

Several scrolls have been broken and repaired on the crest. The frame and crest are painted black over an earlier red.

H. 18½″   W. 9¼″   D. ¾″
(46.99 cm.)   (23.50 cm.)   (1.91 cm.)

PROV. Florene Maine, Ridgefield, Conn.

1954-229

109 LOOKING GLASS
Possibly Boston area
1800–1815
Mahogany and mahogany veneer with
* white pine*

The crest, base, and ears are mahogany, the frame is mahogany veneered on white pine, the backboard is white pine.

Of 1 doz and *22* in ink on backboard. Fragments of old paper, possibly from almanacs, attached to inside of frame.

H. 25½″   W. 13½″   D. ⅞″
(64.77 cm.)   (34.29 cm.)   (2.22 cm.)

PROV. Albert Van de Bunt, Cleveland, O.

An almost identical glass at Winterthur is labeled by the Boston firm of Cermenati and Bernada, who were working in that city in 1807 and 1808.[1] The Winterthur glass differs only in the added feature of three gilt feathers on the crest.

1939-37

1. Montgomery, No. 224.

110

111

111a

110 SIDEBOARD

Probably Connecticut
1790–1810
Cherry with white pine and light and dark
   wood inlays

Most of the inlay defining the cuffs is missing, as are the molded strips above the front legs. The keyhole escutcheons are missing from the side doors; all other brasses are original. The dovetails on the drawers are hidden by an applied strip which also forms the molding surrounding each drawer.

The bails of all brasses are stamped *HJ*.

H. 40″   w. 65½″   D. 28¾″
   (101.60 cm.)   (166.37 cm.)   (73.03 cm.)

The form of this small sideboard is quite usual, the basic design being found in Massachusetts, Connecticut, New York, and New Jersey. In the latter two areas, the front legs are generally canted, while in New England they are usually flat as in this example. Indicative of Connecticut workmanship is the use of cherry as the primary wood and the unusual character of the inlay. The motifs used as inlaid decorations are not in themselves uncommon: the quarter fans, ovals, swastikas, and small shields are found on other Connecticut pieces. What is disturbing is the lack of overall integration of the elements. With the exception of the fans, the motifs seem to be placed at random, wherever there was a blank surface. Also unusual is the lack of contrast between some of the inlaid motifs and the body of the piece itself. In some areas, particularly on the legs and center top drawer, it is almost impossible to distinguish the inlay without the aid of a strong light. All this would seem to point to a craftsman not overly familiar with the use of inlay attempting to dress up an otherwise simple piece for a client.

Anonymous gift
G1971-537

111 SIDE BOARD

Rhode Island
1795–1810
Mahogany and mahogany veneer with
   white pine, tulip, and chestnut

The top and legs are solid mahogany; the other surfaces are mahogany veneered on white pine; the frame is white pine; the drawer sides, back, and bottom are tulip; the blocks beneath the drawers are chestnut. The left side of the case consists of two drawers, one above the other, with the interior of the top drawer divided lengthwise into two equal compartments. The right side of the case consists of one drawer, the front veneered and inlaid to resemble two. The central compartment behind the two doors is plain. All locks are missing from the drawers, the brasses and escutcheons are old but not original, and small brass pulls are missing from the central doors. Some veneer has been patched, and the sides of the large drawer have been built up.

H. 38⅛″   w. 45″   D. 20¼″
   (96.84 cm.)   (114.30 cm.)   (51.44 cm.)

PROV.   John S. Walton, Inc., New York.

Less than a dozen sideboards of this small type have been published. Most are attributed to Providence, Rhode Island, apparently on the basis of one example in the Rhode Island Historical Society attributed to Thomas Howard, Sr.[1] It seems likely that while the production of these pieces may have centered in Providence, they were made elsewhere in that state as well and by a number of craftsmen. Of the several published examples, the most similar example was formerly in the collection of Cornelius C. Moore.[2] Similar in design, the Williamsburg example has the added features of a central inlaid vase on the skirt, from which sprigs of flowers extend, and three-petaled flowers on the face of the front legs. These particular features have not been seen on any other members of the group.

1971-366

---

1. *John Brown Catalog,* No. 48.

2. *Important American Furniture* (New York: Parke-Bernet Galleries, Inc., October 30, 1971), Lot 79.

112 TABLE

Connecticut, Windsor area
1710–30
White pine, maple, and chestnut

The top is white pine, the legs and stretchers are maple, and the feet are chestnut. The table was once covered with a coat of brownish paint. There are tack holes along the edge of the top where some sort of covering was once applied.

H. 23⅜   w. 27⅛   D. 17⅝″
   (60.64 cm.)   (68.90 cm.)   (44.77 cm.)

PROV. Lillian Blankley Cogan, Farmington, Conn.; acquired near Windsor, Conn.

This small table is one of the finest of a limited group of related examples, most of which appear to have Connecticut histories. A very fine example in the Nutting Collection at the Wadsworth Atheneum is similarly constructed but with bolder turnings and the addition of a cross brace beneath the top.[1] Other examples exist, with both rectangular and oval tops.[2]

1963-7

---

1. Kirk, *Connecticut Furniture,* No. 141.
2. Nutting, *Treasury I,* Nos. 1204, 1205, 1211, and 1212.

113 FOLDING TABLE

Maker: Attributed to a member of the Beal
   family
Massachusetts, Hingham area
1720–60
Maple and beech

The top, frame, and gates are maple; the legs, feet, and stretcher are beech. The leaves are hinged with old butterfly hinges, but these are not original to the table. Each gate has had a one-inch channel cut out across the inside surface at the top, and these have subsequently been filled in with wood. This appears to have been done early in the history of the table, as one repair is fastened with a rose-headed nail. The reason for this repair is unclear, but both gates appear to be original. The table was probably painted originally, but no trace of color remains.

H. 25½″   w. 30¼″   D. 29¼″
   (64.77 cm.)   (76.84 cm.)   (74.30 cm.)

PROV. The table descended in the Beal family of Hingham, Mass., to the last private owner, Henry Beale Spelman, Fairfield, Conn.

This is one of two tables in the collection with a strong Hingham, Massachusetts, history (see also No. 129). Several members of the Beal family were wood craftsmen, including John Beal (1657–1735), a carpenter, and John Beal (1730–1814), a cabinetmaker. While it is possible that this table was made by the latter John, the piece is of a style generally thought to have been made earlier in the century.

1955-247

112

113

113a

114

115

114 TABLE
New England
1700–1780
White pine and maple

The top and batten ends are white pine; all other elements are maple. One batten is missing from the top, and the top is split in several places. The legs have been reinforced at the base; the table has been painted white and stripped, but remnants of the original green paint are still visible.

H. 27″   w. 25½″   D. 25½″
(68.58 cm.)   (64.77 cm.)   (64.77 cm.)

PROV. John S. Walton, Inc., New York.

American trestle tables of any form are extremely rare. While the temptation is strong to date all examples in the seventeenth century, this table, at least, was probably made considerably later. Such refinements as the small battens nailed to the top, the crude chamfering of the legs and stretcher, and the rounded shaping of the feet probably indicate a date no earlier than the second quarter of the eighteenth century.

1953-904

115 TABLE
New England
1720–60
White pine, maple, ash, and oak

The top is white pine and is made of two boards secured with battens at the ends; the legs are maple, the sides are ash, and the stretchers are oak. Tack holes are visible along the edges of the top where linoleum or oilcloth was once attached. One top board is split, and the feet have lost some of their height. Remnants of the table's original green paint are still visible.

H. 25⅝″   w. 34¼″   D. 22⅞″
(65.09 cm.)   (87 cm.)   (58.10 cm.)

PROV. Israel Sack, Inc., New York.

This unusual table is reminiscent of Windsor examples of the latter part of the eighteenth century, but the heavy baluster turnings of the legs, the battened top, and the large hand-wrought nails used to secure the sides to the legs and the battens to the top indicate a date earlier in the century. It is difficult to pinpoint a specific provenance for the piece, but the presence of ash may suggest northern New England.

1952-630

116 TABLE

New England
1720–80
Hard maple with white pine

The top, legs, and stretchers are hard maple; the small, dowel-like braces near the top of the legs and the braces beneath the top are white pine. The table is presently covered with a heavy coat of very hard brown varnish, under which the original green paint is visible. The table was originally assembled entirely with pegs; subsequently, nails have been added as reinforcements and many of these are eighteenth-century in date.

H. 22⅛″   w. 24-1/16″   D. 19¼″
   (56.20 cm.)   (61.12 cm.)   (48.90 cm.)

The construction of this small table would seem to indicate a date fairly early in the eighteenth century, but it is extremely difficult to be certain due to the rarity of tables of this sort. Likewise, no specific provenance is indicated by the woods.

Anonymous gift
G1971-555

116

WETHERBURN'S TAVERN, Upper Middle Room

*LOOKING GLASS, New England,
1730–70. (No. 107).*

*TEA TABLE, Probably
New Hampshire, 1730–60.
(No. 128).*

117 TABLE

Probably New England
1720–70
White pine and beech

The top, sides, and brace beneath are white pine, the four legs are beech. One leg has been broken near the top and repaired, and there are several splits in the top, one of which has been repaired by the addition of an old iron brace beneath. The red stain now on the table is not original, but there is evidence of an older coat of red beneath.

H. 26″   w. 29½″   D. 19⅞″
   (66.04 cm.)   (74.93 cm.)   (50.48 cm.)

PROV. Miss Lela Shewmake, Williamsburg, Va.

The presence of beech in furniture is generally thought to indicate a European provenance, but evidence is increasing that American cabinetmakers, particularly in New England, utilized the wood on occasion, generally as a substitute for maple or birch. It is most often seen in combination with other local woods and principally on pieces that were originally painted (in this catalog, see Nos. 41 and 113). This table was discovered in the South and had been attributed to that region. However, the use of white pine and beech and the shaping of the legs (see Nos. 118 and 126) almost surely indicate a New England origin. The scalloping of the skirt is similar to that on several Connecticut chests of the first third of the eighteenth century.[1]

1930-19

117

---

1. Kirk, *Connecticut Furniture,* No. 51

118

119

118 TABLE
New England
1730–70
Maple

The top is made of two boards of unequal size, the smaller of which may be an early replacement. One leg is split near the base.

H. 25¾″   w. 29¾″   D. 22¼″
  (64.41 cm.)   (75.57 cm.)   (56.52 cm.)

PROV. Estate of Mrs. Austin Palmer, Hopkinton, N.H.

The next several pages comprise a related group of small, splay-leg tables of varying design, made principally in the second and third quarters of the eighteenth century. Multipurpose in use, perhaps better than any other form they indicate the simple grace of much New England eighteenth-century furniture. The success of this table is principally attributable to the contrast between the oval top and the straight skirt. The chamfering of the upper leg softens the sharp edges, and the decorative turning below provides a visual transition between the skirt and leg.

1966-422

119 TABLE
Probably New England
1730–70
Maple

This table has suffered a great deal of wear but is basically original. Two feet have been partly replaced, and the legs are split at the top and repaired. The red paint is old but has been touched up in several areas.

H. 25¾″   w. 35¼″   D. 27½″
  (65.41 cm.)   (89.53 cm.)   (69.85 cm.)

PROV. L. G. Myers, New York.

Similar in design to No. 118, this table differs principally in the scalloping of the skirt and the termination of the legs. The unusual flat, sloping feet on high pads are related to those on Hudson Valley chairs of the late eighteenth and early nineteenth centuries,[1] and this table may possibly be of New York origin. In other respects, however, it is related to New England examples and thus is included in this catalog.

1930-77

---

1. Downs, No. 99

120

121

120 TABLE

Possibly Rhode Island
1740–70
Maple

The red paint is old and probably original; the top is warped slightly, and the batten ends are nailed on.

H. 26¼″   W. 30″   D. 18½″
(66.68 cm.)   (76.20 cm.)   (46.99 cm.)

PROV. Teina Baumstone, New York.

The trumpet-shaped, tapering legs on this table are reminiscent of those on Hudson Valley chairs of the second quarter of the eighteenth century. While this similarity may indicate a New York provenance for the table, the flat-headed arches beneath the skirt are characteristic of New England workmanship. A virtually identical table is owned by Mr. and Mrs. Norbert H. Savage.[1] That table, also painted red, is said to have descended in the Cranston family of Rhode Island.

1952-588

---

1. *American Art of the Colonies and Early Republic* (Chicago: Art Institute of Chicago, 1971), No. 17.

121 TABLE

New England
1740–80
Maple

Except for the top, this table is covered with old, brown paint. The top is made of two boards of unequal size.

H. 26½″   W. 28⅞″   D. 22⅜″
(67.31 cm.)   (73.34 cm.)   (56.83 cm.)

PROV. John S. Walton, Inc., New York.

Similar in concept to the previous example, this somewhat smaller table is better integrated. The sharp corners and edges have been rounded off and the legs have more splay, providing a greater feeling of stability.[1]

1955-29

---

1. See Nutting, *Treasury I,* No. 1240, for a similar oval-top table.

122

123

122 TABLE

Probably Connecticut or Rhode Island
1730–1800
Tulip and white pine

The top is tulip, the frame and legs are white pine. The top is made of two boards, originally cleated together from beneath; the cleat is now missing. The table is presently covered with a greenish-black paint under which the original red is visible.

H. 26⅜"   w. 35¼"   D. 26¼"
  (67.63 cm.)   (89.53 cm.)   (66.68 cm.)

PROV. Winick & Sherman, New York.

Tables of this sort were made throughout New England and probably over a long period of time. A Connecticut or Rhode Island attribution for this pristine survival is indicated by the presence of tulip, for this wood is seldom, if ever, found in furniture made north of southern New England. An almost identical table in the Colonial Williamsburg collection is made entirely of maple.

1930-74

123 TABLE

New England
1730–90
Maple

Except for the top, the table is covered with its original dark green paint. Marks on the underside of the top indicate a covering of some sort was once fastened over the edge. The top has warped slightly and there are several small splits at each end.

H. 27"   w. 33¼"   D. 23¼"
  (68.58 cm.)   (84.46 cm.)   (59.05 cm.)

PROV. Philip Flayderman; American Art Association, Anderson Galleries, New York.

PUBL. *Colonial Furniture, Silver & Decorations* (New York: American Art Association, Anderson Galleries, Inc., January 2, 3, and 4, 1930), Lot 276.

Except for the rectangular top, this table is virtually identical to No. 122. Few tables of this form with rectangular tops are known, and it seems likely that the tops of many surviving tables have been cut to an oval shape to conform with twentieth-century taste. That this practice is uncalled for is demonstrated by a close study of this particular table, whose maker took such pains to integrate all of the various elements into an aesthetically pleasing whole.

1930-73

124

125

124 TABLE
New England
1740–80
Maple

The table is currently painted black with previous coats of green and the original red beneath. One foot has been broken and spliced.

H. 26⅛″   w. 33¾″   D. 23½″
(66.36 cm.)   (85.73 cm.)   (59.69 cm.)

PROV.   Roger Bacon Antiques, Exeter, N.H.

This superbly engineered table overcomes most of the design difficulties of the previous two examples. The splay of the legs seems just right to provide stability, and the pad feet are gracefully formed and continue the sweep of the legs themselves. The flat-headed arches lighten the skirt without detracting from the clean lines of the rest of the table.

1961-95

125 TABLE
Possibly Rhode Island
1740–90
Maple

One foot is split and repaired at the ankle, and there are several splits in the top and in one leg at the top. Traces of old red paint remain on the surface.

H. 26¾″   w. 35¼″   D. 27⅛″
(67.95 cm.)   (89.53 cm.)   (68.90 cm.)

PROV.   John S. Walton, Inc., New York.

Tables of this type, known today as porringer tables, probably served as tea, breakfast, or occasional tables in the eighteenth century. They are invariably ascribed to Newport with little apparent documentation, although one example is pictured in a portrait of David Moore of Newport by the artist Samuel King in the collection of Mrs. Edward A. Sherman[1]. The flat, circular feet with a sharp edge running all the way around are very close in design to those on the New Hampshire tea table (No. 128), and it seems likely that tables of this sort were made throughout eastern New England.

1955-28

---

1. William B. Stevens, "Samuel King of Newport," *Antiques* 96 (November 1969), p. 728.

126 TABLE
New England
1740–1800
White pine and maple

The top, skirt, and drawer are white pine; the legs maple. The top is made of three boards secured by narrow battens at each end. The left rear leg is split at the top, and the top shows evidence of heavy wear. The red paint is old but probably not original.

H. 26½″   W. 33¹⁄₁₆″   D. 19″
(67.31 cm.)   (83.98 cm.)   (48.26 cm.)

PROV. Lillian Blankley Cogan, Farmington, Conn.

Tables of this type with a drawer are not seen as frequently as those without drawers. The legs on this example are similar to those on several other tables in this catalog (Nos. 118, 119, and 120), but the moldings lack definition and the foot is tentative and awkwardly conceived.

1953-978

127 TABLE
Probably Connecticut or Rhode Island
1790–1820
White pine, maple, and oak

The top is white pine, the legs and stretchers are maple, the cleats beneath the top are oak. The black paint is not original.

H. 24¼″   W. 34½″   D. 25″
(61.60 cm.)   (87.63 cm.)   (63.50 cm.)

PROV. Henry A. Hoffman, Litchfield, Conn.

The term "Windsor" for tables of this type is apparently of rather recent derivation, for no contemporary references to the term are known to this author. While it is possible that Windsor chairmakers did make tables on occasion, their advertisements invariably mention only chairs and settees. The construction of this table is not unlike that of such items as ladder-back chairs, and it seems likely that the table was crafted by a conventional chairmaker or cabinetmaker rather than a specialist in Windsor furniture.

A specific provenance for this table is difficult to determine. The attribution to Rhode Island or Connecticut is based on the former owner's primary area of collecting.

1952-258

126

127

128

129

128 TEA TABLE
Probably New Hampshire
1730–60
Maple with white pine

The bottom board of the top, the drawer runners, drawer framing, and skirt molding on the sides and rear are white pine; all other areas are maple. The top is made of two boards nailed together flush, each with an applied band of molding attached to all four sides, forming a tray top. The molding around the top has been reattached. Small holes on the inside of each leg indicate wire braces were once attached, and the right rear leg has been broken and repaired. The drawer brass is not original. The entire table is covered with the original red paint.

H. 26½″   w. 31½″   D. 21¼″
   (67.31 cm.)   (80.01 cm.)   (53.98 cm.)

PROV. The table descended in the Treferthen family of Rye and New Castle, N.H. David Stockwell, Inc., Wilmington, Del.

PUBL. *Antiques* 68 (November 1955), front cover; *New Hampshire Arts,* No. 20; Charles E. Buckley, "The Furniture of New Hampshire," *Antiques* 86 (July 1964), p. 57.

Several tables with tray tops, cabriole legs with sharply pointed knees, and flat pad feet are known. A very similar dressing table, with a more deeply scalloped skirt and two drawers rather than one, was formerly in the collection of Mrs. Francis P. Garvan.[1] A rectangular tea table of birch was originally owned by Love Wingate of Hampton, New Hampshire,[2] and a similar example is at Winterthur.[3] The deep hock behind the ankle of each leg is a distinctive feature and may help in identifying further work by the same maker.

1954-502

---

1. *Pilgrim, Queen Anne & Other XVIII Century Furniture* (New York: Parke-Bernet Galleries, Inc., October 31, 1970), Lot 157.
2. *New Hampshire Arts,* No. 15.
3. Downs, No. 366.

129 TEA TABLE
Massachusetts, Boston or South Shore
1740–70
Mahogany with white pine and cedar

The slides are cedar faced with mahogany. Glue blocks beneath the top are white pine; some may not be original. The top has cracked longitudinally and has been tightened by means of several thin blocks screwed to the underside. One foot has been broken and repaired at the ankle. The entire table has been refinished.

Label on underside of top reads: *This table belonged to Daniel Shute, D. D., First Minister in the South Hingham Church.*

H. 26¼″   w. 29¼″   D. 17⅞″
   (66.68 cm.)   (74.29 cm.)   (45.40 cm.)

PROV. Rev. Daniel Shute, Hingham, Mass.; L. G. Myers, New York.

PUBL. *Girl Scouts,* No. 557; *Antiques* 16 (August 1929), p. 113.

In spite of the condition of this table, it remains one of the finest examples of its type known. The delicate top with the notched corners, the elaborately scrolled skirt, the thin, almost straight legs flanked by molded C scrolls—all of these elements combine to produce a table of unparalleled refinement and grace.

The Reverend Daniel Shute, apparently the first owner of the table, was born in Malden, Massachusetts, on July 19, 1722. He graduated from Harvard in the class of 1743 and in 1746 was ordained as the first pastor of the newly organized third parish of Hingham. He remained in the same position until his retirement in 1799, during which period of time he also served as a delegate to the state constitutional convention in 1780 and as a member of the committee which ratified the federal constitution in Massachusetts. He married Mary (daughter of Abel) Cushing of Hingham on March 25, 1753. She died in 1756 and he married again in 1763 Deborah (daughter of Elijah) Cushing of Pembroke. The reverend Shute died in 1802, his wife in 1823. By his first wife, Daniel Shute had one son, Daniel, who graduated from Harvard in 1775 and practiced as a physician in Weymouth and Hingham.

It is impossible to state whether this table was made in Hingham or brought from Boston. Many variants of the type are known, and they were probably made throughout eastern Massachusetts and perhaps into Rhode Island as well. There were at least two cabinetmakers working in Hingham in the middle of the eighteenth century: Elisha Cushing on Main Street and John Beal on East Street.[1] See also No. 113 for another table with a strong Hingham history.

1930-245

1. *History of the Town of Hingham, Massachusetts* (Hingham: n.p., 1893).

130 BREAKFAST TABLE
Probably Massachusetts
1750–90
Mahogany and cherry with white pine and
maple

The table is almost circular when open. The top, legs, and applied ogee skirt of the ends are mahogany, the ends themselves cherry. The body of the table is double walled, the inner walls made of white pine, the outer walls and gates of maple. There are no blocks beneath the top, and no evidence that any were ever there. The four hinges are original, two feet have been broken and repaired, and the table has been refinished.

Handwritten label inside one gate, probably late nineteenth century: *Mrs. Mabel B. Macullas / from / Eliza Y. Sheperd.*

H. 25⅞″	w. open 36⅜″	D. 12¾″
(65.72 cm.)	(92.39 cm.)	(32.39 cm.)

The success of this table is due principally to its proportion and smooth flowing surfaces, broken only by the applied convex molded skirts. The use of cherry on the ends is unusual, and possibly indicates a Connecticut or western Massachusetts provenance.

Anonymous gift
G1971-551

131 BREAKFAST TABLE
Massachusetts, probably Salem area
1770–90
Mahogany with white pine

The gates, frame, and blocks are white pine. The table has been taken apart and reassembled, probably when it was reproduced in the 1950s; new pins fasten both gates. Two feet are split, one bracing block beneath the frame has been replaced, and there are small repairs around two hinges.

H. 26¾″	w. 34″	D. open 40¼″
(67.95 cm.)	(86.36 cm.)	(102.24 cm.)
		D. closed 13¾″
		(34.93 cm.)

PROV. David Stockwell, Inc., Wilmington, Del.

This useful type of table was very common in New England, particularly in eastern Massachusetts and Rhode Island, and occurs in many sizes, both with ball-and-claw and with pad feet (see Nos. 130 and 136). Similar examples with ball-and-claw feet are in the Museum of Fine Arts in Boston[1] and in the collection of Mr. and Mrs. Stanley Stone, and one was formerly owned by H. W. Erving.[2] The sharp knees, which taper quickly to a rounded surface, are generally considered a Salem characteristic (see No. 132).

1951-557

1. Randall, No. 87.
2. Nutting, *Treasury I,* No. 1066.

130

131

132 BREAKFAST TABLE

Massachusetts, Salem area
1750–90
Mahogany with white pine

The frame and gates are white pine. One gate has been taken off and repinned, and the entire table has been refinished.

H. 26⅞″   w. 35⅞″   D. 35″
   (68.26 cm.)   (91.12 cm.)   (88.90 cm.)

PROV.   John S. Walton, Inc., New York.

This table is obviously related to Nos. 130 and 131, but one can see the infinite variations possible. Here the arch of the skirt is much higher, providing an entirely different effect to the table when viewed end on. The form of the legs is the same as No. 131—a sharp knee tapering quickly to a rounded surface, but here the break comes much farther down the leg. Finally, in place of the ball-and-claw foot, the craftsman has utilized a pad foot on a very high disc. This treatment should not be considered an earlier feature. All three tables were almost certainly made within a few years of one another in the same general locality. The decision as to the treatment of the foot was most likely that of the purchaser, who for economic reasons or otherwise preferred the plainer pad. What appears to be an identical table was owned by John S. Walton, Inc., in 1963.[1] A related example in walnut at Winterthur[2] has the same high pad, but the foot is more rounded.

1959-130

1. *Antiques* 83 (April 1963), p. 409.
2. Downs, No. 308.

BRUSH-EVERARD HOUSE, Library

CHEST-ON-CHEST, Massachusetts, Boston or North Shore,
1770–90. (No. 81).

133 DROP-LEAF TABLE

Massachusetts
1750–90
Mahogany with white pine

The fly rail and gate are mahogany, the bracing frame inside the fly rail and the corner blocks white pine. The table was badly damaged several years ago. The right front leg was broken and has been spliced at the top, the left front foot was broken, large repairs were made around both hinges, two large modern blocks were added on the underside to reinforce the top, and holes were drilled through the top when it was reattached.

H. 25⅞″   w. 30¾″   D. open 23⅛″
 (65.72 cm.)   (78.11 cm.)   (58.74 cm.)
                              D. closed 13⅜″
                               (33.97 cm.)

PROV. John S. Walton, Inc., New York.

In spite of its recent damage, this table remains one of the finest examples of a seldom-found type. Similar in design to one at Winterthur,[1] this table lacks the ball-and-claw feet and ogee end skirts of that example. It more than compensates for this, however, by the gracefully formed legs and spreading pad feet, the ogee shaping of the corners of the top, and the serpentine scalloping of the longitudinal rail on the open side. Tables of this form are among the most versatile of all types, for they can be used open or closed, freestanding or against a wall.

1952-573

1. Downs, No. 310.

134 CORNER TABLE

Massachusetts
1740–90
Mahogany with maple and white pine

The hidden frame of the table is maple and the blocks are white pine. The entire table is in its original condition.

H. 27″   W. 35″   D. closed 18″
  (68.58 cm.)   (88.90 cm.)   (45.72 cm.)
                          D. open 34″
                            (86.36 cm.)

PROV. L. G. Myers, New York.

PUBL. *Girl Scouts,* No. 560.

Few forms in American furniture are as pleasing as a well-designed and well-executed corner table. The essentially straight elements of this superb example are skillfully broken by the indentation of the corners of the leaves, the ogee serpentine of the skirt, and the graceful curve of the leg at the knee and ankle. The almost circular, flattened foot resting on a cushion is often found on furniture made in eastern Massachusetts.

1930-227

134

135 GATE-LEG TABLE
Probably Massachusetts
1700–1730
Walnut and white pine

The frame and drawer linings are white pine. The top is slightly warped, and the single drawer is probably a replacement. Casters were once attached to the feet.

H. 27⅜″   W. 40½″   D. open 41⅜″
   (70.17 cm.)   (102.87 cm.)   (105.09 cm.)
                                D. closed 14⅜″
                                 (36.51 cm.)

PROV. John S. Walton, Inc., New York.

PUBL. Milo M. Naeve, "The American Furniture," *Antiques* 95 (January 1969), p. 131.

American, Spanish-footed, gate-leg tables are not common. This example is very close in style to one at Old Deerfield[1] and is similar in many respects to a smaller table at the Wadsworth Atheneum.[2] The feet are particularly well defined.

1959-392

---

1. Comstock, No. 127.
2. Nutting, *Treasury I,* No. 963.

136 DINING TABLE
Massachusetts
1740–90
Mahogany and birch with white pine

The top and skirts are mahogany, the legs birch, and the gates and frame white pine. One gate has been repinned and one leg has been repaired on the inside top edge. The corner blocks of the frame are missing.

H. 27¼″   W. 47⅛″   D. 45¼″
   (69.22 cm.)   (119.70 cm.)   (114.94 cm.)

PROV. Winick & Sherman, New York.

The use of different woods for the top and legs in tables of this sort was apparently quite common and was probably done as an economy measure, for native birch was much less expensive than imported mahogany. The legs were probably stained originally to match the top, and in many cases one must examine a piece carefully to observe the difference. This table closely resembles the much smaller breakfast table (No. 130), but the large, flat feet are closer to those on the corner table (No. 134).

1930-93

135

136

137

138

137 DINING TABLE

Rhode Island, probably Newport
1750–70
Mahogany with maple, chestnut, and
white pine

The gates and frame are maple; the blocks beneath the top are of chestnut and white pine. The underside of the frame is braced by two cross members dovetailed to the frame. Two feet are repaired, and one leg has a long split. Geometric designs are carved inside one end.

H. 30⅜″   W. 68½″   D. open 68¾″
(77.79 cm.)   (173.99 cm.)   (174.63 cm.)
D. closed 20½″
(52.07 cm.)

PROV. John S. Walton, Inc., New York

Several large tables of this type are known. An almost identical example, differing only in its use of pad feet rather than the ball-and-claw, was advertised for sale in 1972.[1] According to family history, that table was owned by John Goddard and used in his house during the Revolution. A second table, with rectangular leaves and pad feet was owned by Israel Sack, Inc., in 1971.[2] All of these tables are characterized by the use of close-grained San Domingo mahogany, simple arched skirts, and virtually straight, cylindrical, tapering legs. This leg treatment is quite unlike the more graceful cabriole seen on another group of Newport dining tables with open claws[3] and is reminiscent of both English furniture and some southern tables.[4] No parallel for the rather awkward, flattened, ball-and-claw foot has been seen, but the shaping of the foot probably resulted from attempting to use it with the rather ungraceful straight leg.

1956-179

---

1. *Antiques* 102 (July 1972), p. 4.
2. *Sack Brochure 20*, No. P3334.
3. *American Art from American Collections* (New York: Metropolitan Museum, 1963), No. 77; *John Brown Catalog*, No. 43.
4. *Antiques* 61 (January 1952), p. 57, Nos. 23, 24; and p. 94, No. 140.

138 DINING TABLE

New England
1790–1810
Cherry with cherry veneer and white pine;
light and dark wood inlay

The table is composed of two semicircular end sections, each with four legs, and a rectangular center section with two leaves and six legs. Each leaf is supported by a gate that swings out on one of the interior legs. The top and legs are cherry, the sides are cherry veneered on built-up strips of white pine, the quarter-round corner blocks are white pine as is the interior framing; the exterior framing of the end sections, the gates, and the cross braces beneath the top of the end sections are cherry. A band of alternating light and dark inlay borders the skirt and extends across the top of each leg. The outside face of all exterior legs is inlaid with vertical stringing in light wood which extends all the way to the floor and is topped by two small leaves of light and dark wood. The hinges to the two drop leaves have been replaced and one gate repaired.

Chalk inscription beneath center section appears to read *J . . . La Fondu Junr.* Inscription appears to be contemporary with table.

H. 28⅜″   L. 105″   D. 47½″
(72.71 cm.)   (266.70 cm.)   (120.65 cm.)

PROV. Philip Flayderman; American Art Association, Anderson Galleries, New York.

PUBL. *Colonial Furniture, Silver and Decorations: The Collection of the Late Philip Flayderman* (New York: American Art Association, Anderson Galleries, Inc., January 2, 3, and 4, 1930), Lot 164.

No information has been discovered about Mr. La Fondu and until something is found it is difficult to attribute this table to a specific area. The use of cherry would seem to indicate Connecticut or western Massachusetts, but the manner in which the stringing on the legs carries all the way to the floor is generally regarded as a Boston or eastern Massachusetts characteristic.

1930-190

139 DINING TABLE

Massachusetts, probably Boston
1805–20
Mahogany with birch and white pine

The gates of each of the three sections are birch, the framing is of white pine. There are no major repairs or restorations and all brass feet and casters are original.

H. 28¼″   L. fully extended   w.56¼″
(71.76 cm.)   179½″   (142.88 cm.)
             (455.93 cm.)

PROV. According to the family history which accompanied this table, it was originally owned by James Hughes (1777–1832) of Baltimore who married Rose Anna Fetter (1793–1891) in 1809 and moved to Louisville, Kentucky, in 1810. At the time of his death, Hughes was president of the United States Bank in Louisville, and the table appears in the inventory of his estate taken the following year as "1 Sett of Dining Tables $40." The table descended in the family until acquired by Colonial Williamsburg.

In spite of the Baltimore and Kentucky history associated with this table, all other evidence points to Boston as the place of manufacture. White pine is seldom used as a secondary wood in Baltimore, and birch is very rarely found in furniture made south of New York. In addition, several very similar tables, all with Boston histories, are known. One example, owned in 1913 by Clinton M. Dyer of Worcester, Massachusetts,[1] supposedly came from the John Hancock home in Boston. A second table, owned by the Society for the Preservation of New England Antiquities in Boston, descended in the family of the founder of that institution, William Sumner Appleton.[2] A third example, although attributed to New York, was said to have formerly been in the possession of a distinguished Boston family.[3] A fourth example also called Boston is pictured in *Antiques*.[4]

1969-227

1. Frances Clary Morse, *Furniture of the Olden Time* (New York: The Macmillan Co., 1913), p. 240.
2. Comstock, No. 568.
3. *Antiques* 81 (January 1962), p. 79.
4. *Antiques* 89 (May 1966), back cover.

139

139a

140

141

142

140 CARD TABLE

Probably Newport, Rhode Island
1770–90
Mahogany with white pine

The back rail and interior blocks are white pine. The gate leg has been broken and repaired where it joins the gate. The surface of the table is marked and scarred in several places.
    Figuring in chalk on rear of gate.

H. 28⅞″   w. 30⅜″   D. open 31½″
 (73.34 cm.)   (77.15 cm.)   (80.01 cm.)
                                 D. closed 15⅞″
                                     (40.32 cm.)

PROV.   Mrs. E. B. Robertson, Petersburg, Va.

Card tables of this type are invariably ascribed to Newport, and most documented examples do have Rhode Island histories. In the finest tables the front skirt is serpentine vertically as well as horizontally, the lower edge of the skirt is finished with a distinct bead rather than with the shallow rope carving, and the legs are generally stop fluted.[1] This was the first antique object acquired by Colonial Williamsburg.

                                    1930-1

———————
1. Carpenter, No. 67.

141 CARD TABLE

Probably Newport, Rhode Island
1785–1800
Mahogany and mahogany veneer with
white pine

The front and sides of the frame are veneered on white pine. The frame and corner blocks are white pine. The interior of the top is plain. The left rear leg swings out to support the top, and behind the gate is a space for a concealed drawer (which is missing). The veneer is cracked and crazed, both rear brackets are missing, the front brackets are replacements copying the two original side brackets. Two of the four corner blocks are replacements. The table has bee. taken apart and reassembled.

H. 28½″   w. 33⅞″   D. open 30⅝″
 (72.39 cm.)   (86.04 cm.)   (77.79 cm.)
                                 D. closed 15¼″
                                     (38.74 cm.)

PROV.   According to information supplied by the donor, the first recorded owner of this table was Dr. Francis Taliaferro Stribling of Staunton, Virginia, who married Henrietta Frances Cuthbert of Norfolk in 1832. Henrietta was the daughter of James and Frances (Bragg) Cuthbert of Norfolk, and Henry Bragg, the father of Frances, had married Diana Wythe Talbot, a niece of the noted lawyer George Wythe of Williamsburg.

The rather poor condition of the table would normally exclude it from a catalog of this sort, but it provides an interesting comparison with No. 140. The frame and top are completely serpentine while the other table has squared corners. The edge of the folding leaf is carved with a series of vertical flutes rather than with thumb moldings, the skirt is veneered, and the molded legs taper rather than maintain their width from top to bottom. Overall, the table is lighter and more graceful than No. 140.

It is certainly coincidental that both of these tables were acquired in Virginia, but this fact again demonstrates the prevalence of Newport furniture in the South in the eighteenth century.
Gift of Mrs. Grace E. Powell, Staunton, Va.
                                  G1956-273.

142 CARD TABLE

Massachusetts, probably Boston or Salem
1805–15
Mahogany with mahogany and figured
birch veneers, cherry, and white pine

One of a pair. The flying rail is black cherry, the framing and blocks are white pine.
    S G.. agg in chalk on inside of rear of frame.

H. 30½″   w. 37¾″   D. 17½″
 (77.47 cm.)   (95.89 cm.)   (44.45 cm.)

PROV.   Ginsburg and Levy, New York.

These tables are apparently the same pair which was sold at the "King Hooper" sale in 1931 where they were assigned to Salem.[1] Two years later, Fiske Kimball published one of the pair as the work of Nehemiah Adams of Salem, basing his attribution on the similarity of the leg treatment to three other tables with a history of ownership in the Adams family.[2] Other tables with similar features have subsequently been published and similarly attributed.[3]

The folly of attempting to attribute all this furniture to a specific maker on the basis of one small detail is illustrated by comparing the leg and foot of these pieces to a dressing table and card table at the Museum of Fine Arts in Boston.[4] The turnings are virtually identical, but the Boston Museum tables are well documented as the work of another Salem maker, William Hook.

The significance of the inscription on the underside of this table has not been determined at this time. One is tempted to relate it to the Boston chairmaker Samuel Gragg, but Gragg's only known productions are the marvelous patented bentwood chairs, examples of which are at Winterthur and the Museum of Fine Arts in Boston.

1971-382, 2

---

1. *XVII and XVIII Century American Furniture* (New York: National Art Galleries, December 3, 4, and 5, 1931), Lot 454.

2. Fiske Kimball, "Salem Furniture Makers II, Nehemiah Adams," *Antiques* 24 (December 1933), p. 220.

3. Montgomery, Nos. 308, 309; *Sack Brochure 10,* No. 540.

4. Randall, Nos. 49, 99.

143 SIDE TABLE
Probably Connecticut
1725–50
Walnut with white pine; marble top

The only elements of secondary wood are small corner blocks of white pine. The skirt on one longitudinal side is cracked; one knee bracket has been repaired, and there are small repairs to the frame and the molded drop heads. The marble top has been broken and repaired at one corner.

H. 28″	W. 58¼″	D. 29″
(71.12 cm.)	(147.96 cm.)	(73.66 cm.)

PROV. Helen Temple Cooke, Wellesley, Mass.; Israel Sack, Inc., New York.

PUBL. Nutting, *Treasury I,* p. 769.

This magnificent table is one of the great pieces of eighteenth-century New England furniture. Nothing is known of its history before the late 1920s except that the name "Governor Saltonstall" has been associated with it since its acquisition by Colonial Williamsburg. Gurdon Saltonstall (1666–1724) was governor of Connecticut from 1708 to 1724. While this table would appear to be too late in date to have been used by him, there may well have been some association with his family.

The table is finished on all four sides, indicating that it was intended to stand in the middle of a room rather than against a wall, and it seems possible that the table was made for a special purpose, perhaps ecclesiastical use.

No similar table of this size is known, but a number of smaller examples of related design have survived. A maple breakfast table at Winterthur has a deeply scalloped skirt reminiscent of this one,[1] as does a small tea or breakfast table owned by Miss Mary Allis of Fairfield, Connecticut.[2] An even closer comparison can be made with the skirt on a high chest from the Woodstock, Connecticut, area which has almost the identical profile, but more tightly compressed.[3] The Williamsburg table was reproduced by Wallace Nutting in the 1930s, and copies are extant.

1930-122

---

1. Downs, No. 352.
2. Kirk, *Connecticut Furniture,* No. 155.
3. Ibid., No. 78.

143

144

144a

144   SIDE TABLE
Probably Massachusetts
1735–70
Mahogany with white pine; marble top

The back rail, corner blocks, and medial brace running from back to front on the underside are white pine. The right rear leg is cracked and repaired at the top. The marble top is original, the underside is rough and unfinished.

H. 27¾″   w. 52¼″   D. 24½″
(70.49 cm.)   (132.72 cm.)   (62.23 cm.)

PROV.   Philip Flayderman; American Art Association, Anderson Galleries, New York.

PUBL.   *Colonial Furniture, Silver and Decoration: the Collection of the late Philip Flayderman.* (New York: American Art Association, 1930), No. 320.

At first glance, this table appears to have the characteristics of a Philadelphia table with its trifid feet and shell-carved knees. Closer examination, however, reveals that the feet, while shaped into three parts, are not formed like the Philadelphia trifid but instead resemble the flat, spreading, Massachusetts pad foot with the corners cut away. The carving of the shells on the skirt and knees does not resemble Philadelphia workmanship either and is actually closer to English or Irish design. The use of white pine as a secondary wood further substantiates a New England attribution, as does the existence of a very similar, but smaller, table at the Jeremiah Lee Mansion in Marblehead, Massachusetts.[1] A gift to the house in 1910, it differs principally in the shaping of the corners and in the use of a pad rather than the trifid foot. The top of the Marblehead table is carved with biblical scenes, which are possibly a later addition, while the underside is unfinished in the same manner as the Williamsburg table. A third table of similar design, also with pad feet but made of walnut, was owned in 1947 by David Stockwell.[2] It was also attributed to Philadelphia.

1930-196

---

1. *Antiques* 63 (January 1953), p. 40.
2. *Antiques* 39 (February 1941), p. 62.

145

145a

145 DRESSING TABLE
Massachusetts
1730–60
Walnut and walnut veneer with white pine

All interior wood is white pine; all flat exterior surfaces are veneered with crotch walnut. The top is made of four matching pieces of veneer framed by two opposed bands in a herringbone pattern surrounded in turn by a broad band of veneer also framed by an outer double herringbone band, the whole terminating in a molded edge. The sides are veneered with two matching panels, and the areas above the legs are separately veneered. Each of the drawer fronts is veneered and bordered with herringbone bands as on the top, and each drawer is framed by a double bead with a channel between. There is no banding on the top of the upper drawer. All brasses are original. The drawer sides and backs are finished with a double arch molding. The face of the skirt is veneered and the skirt is bordered on the front and sides by an applied bead nailed on from beneath. The acorn drops are replacements; the four cabriole legs have pointed knees and taper gracefully to a molded pad foot. Two boards have been attached inside the case on the left side to correct warpage of the veneer.

H. 32¼″ W. 33⅞″ D. 21½″
(81.92 cm.) (86.04 cm.) (54.61 cm.)

PROV. Smith Collection, Winchester, Mass.; Israel Sack, Inc., New York.

PUBL. *Sack Brochure 11,* No. 600; *Sack Brochure 21,* No. P912.

Few New England dressing tables of this quality have survived in such original condition. The interplay of the veneered surfaces, the deep scalloping of the skirt, and the graceful curve of the legs relieve the essentially boxy form. Two other very similar examples are known. One was owned by Major General Benjamin Lincoln of Hingham, Massachusetts.[1] The other, at the Museum of Fine Arts in Boston, is slightly smaller in size.[2] Neither example has the outer double herringbone border that is an integral part of the top of the Williamsburg table.

1972-229

1. *Sack Brochure 22,* No. P3645.
2. Randall, No. 45.

146

146a

146 DRESSING TABLE

Connecticut River Valley
1750–1800
Cherry and white pine

All secondary wood is white pine. The bottom of the central drawer is not original, the brasses are old but not original, and there is a split in the lower edge of the right side.

H. 31⅛″   W. 42″   D. 21⅞″
(79.06 cm.)   (106.68 cm.)   (55.56 cm.)

PROV. L. G. Myers, New York.

PUBL. *Girl Scouts,* No. 564.

This magnificently conceived dressing table is one of the finest examples of New England cabinetmaking in this catalog. Extremely large in scale, it has been given a feeling of great delicacy by the deep scroll carving of the skirt and the superbly curved, tapering legs. Few American craftsmen demonstrated Hogarth's line of beauty as well as the craftsman who fashioned the legs of this piece. Even the back legs, which had to be flattened at the top rear to fit tightly against the wall, demonstrate this graceful flow of line.

It is impossible at this point to assign this table to any one area, but comparisons suggest it was made somewhere in an area between Hartford, Connecticut, and Greenfield, Massachusetts. A table in the Garvan Collection at Yale that was exhibited at the Connecticut furniture show in 1967 has a skirt roughly similar in design to the side skirt on this dressing table,[1] as does a desk in the Barbour Collection at the Connecticut Historical Society.[2] In neither of these pieces, however, is the shaping as well defined as here, and both examples appear weak in comparison.

1930-135

1. Kirk, *Connecticut Furniture,* No. 162.
2. *Frederick M. and Margaret R. Barbour's Furniture Collection* (Hartford: Connecticut Historical Society, 1963), pp.58–59.

147 BUREAU TABLE
Massachusetts, probably Boston
1760–90
Mahogany with white pine

This table has a number of design and construction features not commonly found on other pieces of this type. The side moldings of the top are nailed on rather than carved from the top as is the front molding. The drawers have molded lip edges rather than the applied beads found on most other Massachusetts examples. Behind the central arched door is a removable cupboard section containing a single shelf with cyma-curved front edge. The pair of exposed hinges on the cupboard door is original. This feature has not been seen on other Massachusetts examples, but almost identical hinges are on an attributed New York table at the Albany Institute.[1] There are several minor splits and repairs on the top. All drawer locks are replaced; the brasses are original. The feet have probably lost 1–1½ inches of their original height.

H. 28¾"   W. 32½"   D. 20¼"
(73.03 cm.)   (82.55 cm.)   (51.44 cm.)

PUBL. Nutting, *Treasury I*, No. 264; *Antiques* 13 (June 1928), p. 462; *The Art Quarterly* 22 (Autumn 1959), p. 278.

This table is an interesting variant on a conventional Massachusetts form. The bold rounded blocking of the drawer fronts is emphasized by the beautifully matched grain of the wood. The brasses are set unusually high on the drawers, apparently so as not to hide the pronounced figure of the wood. A number of similar Boston examples with both round and flat blocking are known, but none exactly matches this particular piece.[2]

Gift of Mrs. Francis P. Garvan
G1958-627

1. Nancy A. Goyne, "The Bureau Table in America," *Winterthur Portfolio III* (Winterthur, Del.: 1967), p. 32.

2. The most nearly similar example is pictured in Sack, *Fine Points,* p. 151.

147

148 WINDSOR ARMCHAIR
Probably Rhode Island
1780–1800
Maple, white pine, and ash

The baluster arm supports, legs, and stretchers are maple, the seat is white pine, and the arm rails and bow are ash. The left rear leg is split and has been repaired, the medial stretcher is split on the right side, and the left side of the seat has split and been repaired. The terminals of the arms are separate pieces which have been nailed to the ends of the arm rails. The chair is covered with a blue-green paint, and traces of an earlier red are visible beneath.

H. 37″   W. 16¾″   D. 17″
  (93.98 cm.)   (42.55 cm.)   (43.18 cm.)

PROV. L. G. Myers, New York.

PUBL. *Girl Scouts*, No. 526.

Chairs like this—with a continuous arm rail terminating in vertical scrolls, baluster-turned spindles, and legs that taper sharply at the bottom—have traditionally been ascribed to Rhode Island, although, as far as this writer is aware, no documented Rhode Island Windsors of this type are known. Of particular note is the crispness and definition in the turnings of the spindles, arm supports, and legs.

1930-64

149 WINDSOR ARMCHAIR
Probably Rhode Island
1780–1800
Maple, mahogany, white pine, and ash

The legs, stretchers, and arm supports are maple, the arms are mahogany, the seat is white pine, the bow and spindles are ash. The bow is split on the left side where it joins the end spindle. The chair is presently painted black, but remnants of the original green are visible beneath.

H. 38¼″   W. 18⅛″   D. 17⅝″
  (97.16 cm.)   (46.04 cm.)   (44.77 cm.)

PROV. Henry A. Hoffman, Litchfield, Conn.

PUBL. Nancy A. Goyne, "American Windsor Chairs: A Style Survey," *Antiques* 95 (April 1969), p. 542, fig. 10.

In contrast to No. 148, which this example closely resembles, the turned members here are weak and ill-defined, thus giving a thin and elongated character to the chair. In addition, the arms, instead of being continuous extensions of the bow, are entirely separate members. The use of separate mahogany arms seems to be confined to bow-back Windsors of this type, and they are generally credited to Rhode Island, although no firm documentation for this attribution has been found.

1952-256

150 WINDSOR ARMCHAIR
Probably Rhode Island
1780–1800
Maple, mahogany, white pine, and ash

The arm supports, legs, and stretchers are maple, the arms are mahogany, the seat is white pine, and the bow and spindles are ash. The right arm support is split slightly. Traces of original green paint are visible beneath the present black.

H. 38⅜″   W. 17⅛″   D. 19¾″
  (97.47 cm.)   (43.50 cm.)   (50.16 cm.)

PROV. Henry A. Hoffman, Litchfield, Conn.

Acquired with No. 149, this example is identical with the exception of the addition of two bracing spindles to the back. A set of twelve very similar chairs, branded *A. G. Case,* was owned by Peter Tillou of Litchfield, Connecticut, in 1969.[1] A single chair, virtually identical in form, is in the collection of Stanley Stone.[2]

1952-257

1. *Antiques* 96 (October 1969), p. 453.
2. *Antiques* 91 (February 1967), p. 211.

148

149

150

151

152

153

151 WINDSOR SIDE CHAIR
Possibly Rhode Island
1780–1800
Maple, white pine, and ash

The legs and stretchers are maple, the seat is white pine, and the bow and spindles are ash. Now painted black, the chair displays evidence of the original green. This chair is one of a pair in the Colonial Williamsburg collection.

Cole written in red crayon beneath seat.

H. 39⅞″   W. 16″   D. 19⅛″
(101.28 cm.)   (40.64 cm.)   (48.58 cm.)

PROV. L. G. Myers, New York

PUBL. *Girl Scouts,* No. 529.

Similar in design to the preceding examples, the turnings here are even weaker, and the chair appears spindly. Side chairs were not made as early as arm chairs and, particularly in this bow-back form, are generally less successful in design.

1930-104, 1

152 WINDSOR SIDE CHAIR
Probably Rhode Island
1785–1800
Maple, white pine, and hickory

This chair is one of a pair in the Williamsburg collection. The legs and stretchers are maple, the seat is white pine, and the bow and spindles are hickory. The chairs were originally painted green, but now are covered with black. Part of the original green wool upholstery is still attached to the chair beneath a later covering.

H. 38¼″   W. 17¾″   D. 18¾″
(97.16 cm.)   (45.09 cm.)   (47.62 cm.)

PROV. Mr. Walter M. Schwartz, Jr., Philadelphia, Pa.

Comparatively few upholstered Windsor chairs have survived, although the variation seems to have been quite popular in the latter years of the eighteenth century. Most surviving examples can be attributed to New York, where the fashion apparently originated. Thomas and William Ash, Windsor chairmakers at 17 John Street, advertised in 1785 that they were making "very neat Chairs and Settees, some of which is very elegant, being stuffed in the seat and brass nailed, a mode peculiar to themselves, and never before executed in America...."[1] This particular braced-back example is significant for the retention of part of its original upholstery and stuffing. The style of the turnings is very similar to that of Nos. 148 through 151, indicating a probable Rhode Island provenance. A virtually matching pair of armchairs was advertised for sale in 1961.[2]

1958-4

_____
1. *New York Packet,* March 3, 1785, as quoted in Rita Susswein Gottesman, *The Arts and Crafts in New York, 1777–1797* (New York: New York Historical Society, 1954), p. 110.
2. *Antiques* 79 (March 1961), p. 236.

153 WINDSOR SIDE CHAIR
Probably Connecticut
1780–1800
Maple, hickory, and sycamore

The legs and front stretchers are maple, the bow, spindles, side and rear stretchers are hickory, and the seat is sycamore. The seat is split in several places and the legs have lost approximately two inches at the base. The chair has been painted green several times.

H. 38⅜″   W. 17½″   D. 20¼″
(97.48 cm.)   (44.45 cm.)   (51.44 cm.)

PROV. Israel Sack, Inc., New York.

This chair is highly unusual in a number of features. The legs, while of conventional form and similar to those on No. 152, are much heavier than normal on chairs of this type. The arrangement and shaping of the stretchers may well be unique, and the use of sycamore for the seat has been seen on only one other example. The combination of these unusual features leads one to consider Connecticut as a probable point of origin for this chair. That supposition is further strengthened by the lack of a groove in the seat in front of the spindles (what appears to be a groove in the photograph is a painted line to simulate such a groove, added at a later date) and the fact that the legs do not extend through the seat.

1952-173

154

155

156

156a

154 WINDSOR ARMCHAIR
Probably Connecticut or Rhode Island
1780–1800
Maple, tulip, and ash

The arms, arm supports, legs, and stretchers are maple, the seat is tulip, and the bow and spindles are probably ash. The scrolls of the ends of the arms are made as separate pieces and are pinned through the top of the arm. The chair is presently painted black; remnants of the original green are visible beneath.

H. 40⅜″   w. 19⅛″   D. 15¼″
(102.55 cm.)   (48.58 cm.)   (38.74 cm.)

PROV. L. G. Myers, New York.

PUBL. *Girl Scouts,* No. 531.

Chairs of this type, called "sack back" in the eighteenth century, were made in Philadelphia as well as New England. The elongated proportions of this chair along with the generous saddling of the seat indicate a New England provenance, and the presence of tulip in the seat and the sharp taper at the bottom of the legs suggest Connecticut or Rhode Island as a likely source. A related example is branded by Amos D. Allen of Norwich, Connecticut.[1]

1930-62

----

1. Nancy A. Goyne, "American Windsor Chairs: A Style Survey," *Antiques* 95 (April 1969), p. 541.

155 WINDSOR ARMCHAIR
Probably Connecticut or Rhode Island
1780–1800
Maple, white pine, and ash

The legs, stretchers, and arm supports are maple, the seat is white pine, and the bow and spindles are ash. The scrolls at the ends of the arms are made as separate pieces as in No. 154. The right arm support has been reinforced by a brass rod inserted through from beneath the seat; several of the ring turnings on the legs and stretchers have been chipped. The chair was originally painted green, but later coats of red, blue, and black are visible.

H. 43¼″   w. 21¾″   D. 15⅞″
(109.86 cm.)   (55.25 cm.)   (40.32 cm.)

PROV. L. G. Myers, New York.

PUBL. *Girl Scouts,* No. 528.

This chair is very similar to the preceding example but lacks the added crest on the arm rail and the sharp taper at the base of the legs. The seat is not as well shaped, and the arms, though well formed, do not flare out as far to the side.

1930-65

156 WINDSOR ARMCHAIR
Maker: Samuel Jones Tuck
Boston, Massachusetts
1790–1800
Maple, white pine, and ash

The arm rail, arm supports, legs, and stretchers are maple; the seat is white pine; the bow and spindles are ash. The chair is covered with a coat of modern red paint over the original green.

Brand beneath seat: *S. J. TUCKE.* Paper label beneath seat: *This chair was made by S. J. Tucke / Cornhill, Boston, Mass. where / name appeared in Boston / Directory as manufacturer of / chairs up to 1760 when it ceased / showing that it must be at least / that old. Given to my father / in the 1860s by the Seargent of / Arms at the Mass. State House when / he represented Chelsea in the / legislature as "Speaker John Hancock's / chair."*

H. 37⅝″   w. 21″   D. 16¼″
(95.57 cm.)   (53.34 cm.)   (41.28 cm.)

PROV. Richard L. Mills, Exeter, N.H.

Samuel J. Tuck advertised in the *Massachusetts Centinel* in March 1790: "Windsor chairs of the newest and most elegant fashions, warranted superior to any exposed for sale elsewhere in Boston, and upon as reasonable terms, ready made, or furnished upon the shortest notice by SAMUEL JONES TUCK, Kilby Street, who returns his most unfeigned thanks to his friends and the public for the favors he has experienced...." From this ad it is evident that Tuck had been working previous to this date, but he is not listed in the first Boston directory of 1789. No further advertisements of his have been found, but he is listed in the 1796 Boston directory as proprietor of a "Windsor Chair Manufactory" on Batterymarch Street. In the U. S. Direct Tax of 1798, Samuel Tuck, Edward and William Hay, William Burroughs, and others were the occupants of "1 wooden building 70 × 24, 3 stores, chair maker, Sail do. and C & C, 4200 square feet."

Tuck's name is consistently spelled without an *e* in all of the printed sources, but his brand, which appears beneath the seat of this chair and on another bamboo-turned, bow-back chair which this writer has examined, very clearly has an *e*.

The history given on the nineteenth-century label attached to the chair is probably erroneous, at least in part. John Hancock died in 1793 while serving as governor and could conceivably have owned the chair, but it seems doubtful a chair of this type would have been used by him in any official capacity. More likely, it was used in the Massachusetts State House during the nineteenth century when a false tradition was attached to it.

1970-129

157 WINDSOR SIDE CHAIR
Probably Rhode Island or eastern
Connecticut
1785–1800
Maple, white oak, and tulip

The legs, stretchers, and posts are maple, the bow and spindles are white oak, and the seat is tulip. At least two coats of dark red paint cover the original green.

An obscure signature *W*....... is written in white chalk beneath the seat.

H. 35¼″   w. 17⅜″   D. 16⅜″
  (89.53 cm.)   (44.13 cm.)   (41.59 cm.)

PROV. Herbert Schiffer, Exton, Pa.

The provenance of this chair, which was acquired in Pennsylvania, has been open to some debate. The swelled tapering of the legs is typical of chairs attributed to Rhode Island. The floatlike swell of the side stretchers also appears to be an eastern New England characteristic.[1]

1966-509

———

1. See a chair at Winterthur branded by Amos D. Allen of Norwich, Connecticut, illustrated in Nancy A. Goyne, "American Windsor Chairs: A Style Survey," *Antiques* 95 (April 1969), p. 541.

158 WINDSOR ARMCHAIR
Maker: C. Chase
New England
1780–1800
Maple, tulip, and ash or hickory

The posts, legs, and stretchers are maple, the seat, tulip, and the crest rail, arms, and spindles are ash or hickory. The entire chair is covered with modern red paint over an earlier black and the original green. The arm scroll is made of a single piece, the arms are pinned with nails at the back of the stiles, and a separate tail piece is tenoned and pinned to the seat to support the braces.

Brand beneath seat at front within rectangular border: *C Chase.*

H. 47¾″   w. 22⅞″   D. 21¼″
  (121.29 cm.)   (58.10 cm.)   (53.98 cm.)

PROV. Henry A. Hoffman, Litchfield, Conn.

C. Chase, the maker of this fan-back Windsor armchair, has not yet been identified. Braceback chairs of this type are characteristic of New England workmanship, however, and the tulip seat would seem to indicate Rhode Island or Connecticut. Another chair branded by the same maker and identical in all respects is at Winterthur.[1]

1952-259

———

1. Nancy A. Goyne, "American Windsor Chairs: A Style Survey," *Antiques* 95 (April 1969), p. 542, fig. 11.

157

158

158a

159

159a

160

159 WINDSOR WRITING-ARM CHAIR

Maker: Ebenezer Tracy
Lisbon, Connecticut
1770–1803
Maple, white pine, chestnut, and oak

The arm rail, arm supports, legs, and stretchers are maple, the drawers, slide, and writing arm are white pine, the seat is chestnut, and the spindles are white oak. When acquired, the chair was covered with a very heavy coat of dark brown varnish, which has been removed revealing the original dark green paint. Casters were once attached to the bottom of each foot.
Branded *EB:TRACY* beneath seat.

H. 31¾″	W. 36½″	D. 30½″
(80.65 cm.)	(92.71 cm.)	(77.47 cm.)

PROV. Acquired by the donor in East Orange, N.J.

This chair is one of the finest of the many branded Tracy chairs known, and one of the most successful and complete among the few surviving writing-arm Windsors. It compares favorably with a virtually identical chair in the Garvan Collection at Yale that has the added feature of a crest.[1] This chair appears never to have had a crest.

Ebenezer Tracy was born in Lisbon, Connecticut, in 1744 and died there in 1803. Included in his inventory, the value of which was over $8,200, were a writing chair and cushion, 8 cushioned bottomed chairs, 6 yellow chairs, 22 green chairs, 1 large fiddle-back chair, 6,400 chair rounds and legs, 277 chair bottoms, 148 feet of mahogany, cherry, birch, and beech, also pine, whitewood, maple, and chestnut boards, molding tools, joiner planes, chisels, gauges, and other tools. It seems obvious from this large stock and from the large number of surviving branded examples that Tracy was one of the most prolific of the early Windsor chairmakers.[2]

Anonymous gift
G1971-507

1. Kirk, *Connecticut Furniture*, No. 249.
2. For further information on Tracy's career see Ada R. Chase, "Ebenezer Tracy: Connecticut Chairmaker," *Antiques* 30 (December 1936), pp. 266–69.

160 WINDSOR WRITING-ARM CHAIR

Probably Connecticut
1780–1800
Birch, white pine, tulip, and white oak

The legs, stretchers, and arm posts are birch, the seat is tulip, the writing arm, drawers, and slide are white pine, and the crest, arm rail, and spindles are white oak. The chair is presently covered with a yellow grained paint, probably dating from early in the nineteenth century. There appears to be a dark green or black paint in places beneath the present coat. The joint between the arm rail and the writing arm has been repaired, and the pull on the drawer beneath the seat is a replacement.

H. 42″	W. 34⅜″	D. 15½″
(106.68 cm.)	(87.31 cm.)	(39.37 cm.)

PROV. Lillian Blankley Cogan, Farmington, Conn.; discovered in Saybrook, Conn.

Seldom is one better able to observe the differences between a good chair and a great one than by comparing this writing-arm Windsor with No. 159. Although the chair pictured here is fitted with a crest, a highly desirable feature, it is inferior to No. 159 in every other way. The turnings of the legs and arm supports, although similar in design, lack the sharpness and grace of those on the Tracy chair. The drawer beneath the seat is too deep, giving the chair a bottom-heavy appearance. The arm rail is very thin visually, particularly where it joins the writing arm, and in fact, the break at that point indicates it did not meet well its intended use. The Tracy chair, on the other hand, has a massive rail, further strengthened by an added support, but so lightened as to mask any indication of massiveness. Notice also the gracefulness of the spindles in the Tracy chair, which swell strongly at the center, while in this chair the maker almost seemed to be trying to disguise the swellings and succeeded only in making them heavy and unattractive.

1963-8

161

161a

162

161 WINDSOR ARMCHAIR
Maker: W. Zutphen
Probably New England, possibly
Connecticut or Rhode Island
1810–30
Maple, tulip, and ash or hickory

The legs are maple, the seat is tulip, all other elements are hickory or ash. The chair is presently painted a deep red, beneath which are several earlier coats, the bottom one of which appears to be black.
W. ZUTPHEN branded beneath seat.

H. 34″   w. 19¾″   D. 16¾″
(86.36 cm.)   (50.16 cm.)   (42.55 cm.)

The maker of this bamboo-turned chair has not yet been identified. The slimness of the legs and well-shaped seat indicate a New England origin. The presence of tulip would seem to suggest Connecticut or Rhode Island as a possible provenance.

Anonymous gift
G1971-586

162 WINDSOR BENCH
New England
1810–40
Birch and white pine

The seat is white pine, all other elements are birch. The black paint with gilt decoration is original. A footrest formerly doweled between the front legs is missing.

H. 33¼″   w. 24⅝″   D. 11¾″
((84.46 cm.)   (62.55 cm.)   (29.84 cm.)

Probably custom-made to seat twins, this unusual bench is a rare survival in nineteenth-century Windsor furniture.

Anonymous gift
G1971-504

163

164

163 BABY CAGE
New England
1730–1800
White pine

Part of the seat has been broken off. With this exception the piece is in excellent condition and retains its original gray-green paint.

H. 20″   w. 21½″   D. 21½″
(50.80 cm.)   (54.61 cm.)   (54.61 cm.)

Several cages of this type have been found in New England.[1] There is no evidence that this example ever had casters, and it was apparently intended as a combination playpen and chair. Although no European examples of this form have been seen, a similar cage on wheels is pictured in a late sixteenth-century French wood engraving.[2]

Gift of Harry E. Damon
G1949-287

———

1. Nutting, *Treasury I,* No. 1431; *Antiques* 77 (February 1960), p. 182; and 83 (May 1963), p. 519.

2. Henry René d'Allemagne, *Histoire des Jouets* (Paris: Librairie Hachette & Cie., 1902), p. 25.

164 LETTER RACK
New England
1835
White pine

The piece is nailed and pegged together; no dovetails were used. Much of the surface is still covered with the original yellow-green paint. A wooden rod apparently once extended across the back of the top and was doweled through holes in the saw-toothed fret; nail holes across the top of the front possibly indicate a cloth once hung down covering the rack opening. The bottom of the left front foot is a replacement. Modern hanging hooks have been attached at the rear, but the piece was apparently originally intended to stand on a flat surface rather than to be hung.

1835 painted in yellow on base.

H. 30½″   w. 25¼″   D. 9⅝″
(52.07 cm.)   (64.14 cm.)   (24.45 cm.)

PROV. Avis and Rockwell Gardiner, Stamford, Conn.

This small, useful rack is a superb example of "country furniture." The date on the base seems to be painted in the same pigments as the surface of the rack itself and is probably contemporary with it.

1950-144

Index

Index

Numbers refer to catalog entries.

A

Abby Aldrich Rockefeller Folk Art Collection, 58
Adams, James, 84
Adams, Nehemiah, 142
Albany Institute, 147
Albany (New York), 79
Alexander. *See* Stone and Alexander
Allen, Amos D., 154, 157
Allen, Charles, 61
Allis, Miss Mary, 143
Ames, William, 83
Andover (Massachusetts), 54, 55
Appleton, William Sumner, 139
Art Institute of Chicago, 72
Ash, Thomas, 152
Ash, William, 152

B

Babcock, Samuel G., 83
Back stool, 61, 62
Baltimore (Maryland), 139
Baltimore Museum of Art, 80
Barbour Collection, 96, 146
Barre (Vermont), 106
Bayou Bend Collection, 33, 80
Beal family, 113
Beal, John, 113, 129
Beds: child's, 5; field, 18; folding, 19-21; low-post, 1-5; tall-post, 6-17
Bench, Windsor, 162
Benjamin, A., 101
Beverly (Massachusetts) Historical Society, 3
Bigelow, Anna (Earle), 106
Bigelow, Ithamer, 106
Bigelow, Lewis, 106
Bigelow, Persis, 106
Bigelow, Persis (Barrett), 106
Bigelow, Timothy, 106
Blair, Mrs. J. Insley, 8, 33, 102
Bolles Collection, 80

Bombé furniture, 81
Bookcase, 93
Booth, Ebenezer, 82
Booth, Elijah, 82
Booth, Joel, 82
Boston furniture: bureau table, 147; chairs, 40, 50, 54, 156; chests, 80, 81; clocks, 84; desks, 98, 100; looking glass, 109; secretary, 104; tables, 129, 139, 142, 147; Windsor chairs, 156
Bostonian Society, 3
Bowen, Nathan, 81
Bragg, Henry, 141
Brewster family, 80
Bridgewater (Connecticut), 78
Bright, George, 81, 98
Brookline (Massachusetts), 53
Brown, Gawen, 83
Brown, G. Winthrop, 83
Brown (John) House, 3, 52
Brown, Moses, 3, 51
Brown, Moses, school, 51
Brush-Everard House (Williamsburg), 8
Bulkley, David, 58
"Bull," 91
Bunn, Peter, 79
Burroughs, William, 156

C

Cabinetmakers: Adams, Nehemiah, 142; Allen, Amos D., 154, 157; Allen, Charles, 61; Ash, Thomas, 152; Ash, William, 152; Beal, John, 113, 129; Bigelow, Lewis, 106; Booth, Ebenezer, 82; Booth, Elijah, 82; Booth, Joel, 82; Bowen, Nathan, 81; Bright, George, 81, 98; Bulkeley, David, 58; Case, A. G., 150; Chase, C., 158; Cogswell, John, 81; Cushing, Elisha, 129; Davis, Robert, 80; Fowler, Richard, 61; Frothing-

ham, Benjamin, 98; Gaines family, 86; Gardner, 68; Goddard, John, 51, 137; Gould, John Jr., 77; Gragg, Samuel, 142; Hall, Eli, 82; Hook, William, 89, 142; Howard, Thomas Sr., 111; Ince and Mayhew, 61; Johnson, Edmund, 64; King, William, 102; Long, William, 38; Manwaring, Robert, 55; Martin, Ebenezer, 81; Noyes, Samuel, 77; Pimm, John, 80; Poor, Enoch, 103; Ruggles, Levi, 77; Seymour, John, 77, 104; Seymour, Thomas, 104; Small, Jonathan, 71; Stone & Alexander, 100; Townsend, Job, 52, 87; Townsend, John, 83, 99; Tracy, Ebenezer, 159; Tuck, Samuel Jones, 156; Warner, Reuben, 78; Zutphen, W., 161
Cage, baby, 163
Candlestands, 22-28
Carnegie Institute Museum of Art, 81
Carr House, 9
Carr, Samuel, 9
Case, A. G., 150
Cermenati and Bernada, 109
Chairs: arm, 29, 30, 33-37, 39, 44, 46; back stool, 61, 62; "Boston," 40; "Brewster," 29; "Carver," 29; corner, 60; easy, 66-69; export of, 40; "Go," 38; high, 31-32; invalid, 38; lolling, 63; "Martha Washington," 63-64; "New England," 40; side, 40-43, 45, 47-59; upholstered arm, 63-65; Windsor, 148-161
Charleston (South Carolina), 7, 8, 61
Charlestown (Massachusetts), 98
Chase, C., 158
Chatham (Massachusetts), 71
Chelsea (Massachusetts), 156
Chester (Vermont), 100
Chests: apothecary, 78; blanket, 73; bombé, 81; of drawers, 74-75, 77;

of drawers, high, 76, 78-82; japanned, 80; Taunton, 72; with drawers, 70-72

Claggett, William, 83

Clark, T., 73

Clockmakers: Brown, Gawen, 83; Claggett, William, 83; Creak, William, 83; Dodge, Seril, 83; Storrs, Marmaduke, 83; Wady, James, 83; Willard, Aaron, 84; Willard, Aaron Jr., 85; Willard, Simon, 85

Clocks: Banjo, 85; Tall-case, 83, 84

Clough (William) House, 3

Cogswell, John, 81

"Cole," 151

Collectors and Collections: Abby Aldrich Rockefeller Folk Art Collection, 58; Albany Institute, 147; Allis, Miss Mary, 143; Ames, William, 83; Babcock, Samuel G., 83; Baltimore Museum of Art, 80; Barbour Collection, 96, 146; Bayou Bend Collection, 33, 80; Beverly (Massachusetts) Historical Society, 3; Blair, Mrs. J. Insley, 33, 102; Boston Museum of Fine Arts, 36, 47, 50, 53, 55, 77, 81, 87, 89, 98, 99, 131, 142, 145 (Karolik Collection, 98, 99); Bostonian Society, 3; Brown, G. Winthrop, 83; Carnegie Institute Museum of Art, 81; Chicago, Art Institute of, 72; Currier Gallery of Art, 103; Detroit Institute of Arts, 81; Dyer, Clinton M., 139; Erving, Henry Wood, 57, 131; Essex Institute, 55, 81; Flayderman, Benjamin, 77; Flayderman, Philip, 50, 52; Ford Museum, 83, 100; Garvan Collection, *see* Yale University; Garvan, Mrs. Francis P., 50, 128; Gunther, John J., 82; Jeremiah Lee Mansion, 144; Litchfield Historical Society, 96; Little, Mrs. Nina Fletcher, 1, 102; Marvin, James W., 82; Massachusetts Historical Society, 55; Metropolitan Museum of Art, 29, 68, 80, 83 (Bolles Collection, 80); Moore, Cornelius C., 64, 111; Moses Brown School, 51; New Haven Colony Historical Society, 80; Newport Historical Society, 52; Old Deerfield, 98, 135; Old State House, Boston, 53; Old Sturbridge Village, 38, 50; Page,

Blin W., 53; Rhode Island Historical Society, 111; Rhode Island School of Design, 104; Robb, Mrs. Walter B., 6; Seymour, George Dudley, 34; Sherman, Mrs. Edward A., 125; Smith Collection, 145; Society for the Preservation of New England Antiquities (SPNEA), 139; Stone, Mr. and Mrs. Stanley, 131, 150; Wadsworth Atheneum, 135; Nutting Collection, 112; Winterthur, Henry Francis du Pont, Museum, 6, 7, 16, 33, 48, 52, 55, 64, 65, 77, 80, 82, 83, 87, 100, 104, 109, 132, 133, 142, 143, 158; Yale University, Garvan Collection, 2, 36, 37, 47, 146, 159

"Command," 80

Connecticut furniture: beds, 10, 16, 17; candlestands, 25; chairs, 34, 36, 37, 39, 46, 57, 58; chests, 70, 73, 78, 79, 82; cupboards, 91; desks, 96; sideboards, 110; tables, 112, 122, 127, 143; Windsor chairs, 153-155, 157, 159, 161

Connecticut River Valley, 146

Cooke family, 99

Coombs, L. B., 84

Copley, John Singleton, 61

Cranston family, 120

Creak, William, 83

Cupboards: bookcase, 93; cupboard desk, 92; dresser, 90; hanging, 91

Currier Gallery of Art, 103

Cushing, Abel, 129

Cushing, Deborah, 129

Cushing, Elisha, 129

Cushing, Lucy, 94

Cushing, Mary, 129

Cushing, Rev. James, 94

Cuthbert, Frances Bragg, 141

Cuthbert, Henrietta Frances, 141

Cuthbert, James, 141

D

Dane family, 54, 55

Davis, Robert, 80

Daybeds, 86, 87

Dealers: Ahern, Mrs. W. S., 53; Arons, Harry, 7; Bacon, Roger, 15, 16, 22, 33, 35, 39, 124; Baumstone, Teina, 2, 120; Bradley, Philip H., Co., 13; Brockwell, Mrs. B. L., 105; Byard, John Kenneth, 3, 17, 78; Cogan, Lillian

Blankley, 5, 70, 91, 107, 112, 126, 160; Cushman, Franklin, 37; Gardiner, Avis & Rockwell, 164; Ginsburg and Levy, 44, 58, 142; Good and Hutchinson, 100; Hammitt, Kenneth, 82; Hammond, Roland B., Inc., 54, 55; Kernodle, George, 43; Maine, Florene, 36, 108; Mills, Richard L., 156; Navis, Charles, 34, 46; Osborns, the Earl B., 68; Pottinger, David, 82; Robertson, Mrs. E. B., 140; Sack, Israel, Inc., 1, 3, 11, 14, 18, 20, 31, 52, 74, 84, 85, 88, 90, 93, 94, 98, 104, 115, 143, 145, 153; Schiffer, Herbert, 157; Stallings, Willis, 56; Stockwell, David, Inc., 19, 21, 24, 86, 128, 131; Trump, R. T. and Co., 7; Ullman, Mrs. Lawrence J., 4; Van de Bunt, Albert, 109; Van Rensselaer, Stephen, 38; Walton, John S., Inc., 6, 9, 10, 12, 25, 41, 42, 62-65, 80, 87, 92, 111, 114, 121, 125, 132, 133, 135, 137; Williams Antique Shop, 61; Winick & Sherman, 27, 28, 103, 122, 136

Dennis family, 9, 11

Desks, 94-100, 106. *See also* Secretaries

Detroit Institute of Art, 81

Dodge, Seril, 83

Dressers. *See* Cupboards

Dyer, Clinton M., 139

E

Earls, William, 98

East Orange (New Jersey), 159

Eddy family, 87

Ellery family, 11, 50

Elmendorf, Elizabeth (van Rensselaer), 79

Elmendorf, Maria, 79

Elmendorf, Peter Edmund, 79

Erving, Henry Wood, 57, 131

Essex County (Massachusetts), 81

Essex Institute, 55, 81

F

Fairbanks, Mrs. F. E., 100

Fairfield (Connecticut), 34, 58

Falmouth (Maine), 71

Farmington (Connecticut), 58

Fayetteville (North Carolina), 105

Fetter, Rose Anna, 139

Flayderman, Benjamin, 77

Numbers refer to catalog entries.

Flayderman, Philip, 50, 52
Ford, Museum, 83, 100
Fowler, Richard, 61
Frothingham, Benjamin, 98
Fuessnich, Fred, 31
Fuller, L. R., 100

G

Gaines family, 86
Gardner, 68
Garvan Collection, 2, 36, 37, 47, 146, 159
Garvan, Mrs. Francis P., 128
Gerry, Elbridge, 53
Girl Scout Loan Exhibition, 48-49, 51, 54, 60, 66, 129, 134
Gloucester (Massachusetts), 50, 146, 148, 151, 154-155
Goddard, John, 51, 137
Gould, John Jr., 77
Gragg, Samuel, 142
Grant family, 100
Grant, Moses, 100
Greenfield (Massachusetts), 146
Gunther, John J., 82

H

H J, 110
Hadley, Francis C., 100
Halford, Mr. and Mrs. John, 1
Hall, Eli, 82
Hampton (New Hampshire), 128
Hancock, John, 139, 156
Hanford, Mrs. Ernest J., 45
Hartford (Connecticut), 146; price list of 1792, 14
Harvard College, 94
Harwich (Massachusetts), 71
Haverhill (Massachusetts), 94
Hay, Edward, 156
Hay, William, 156
"Hill," 91
Hingham (Massachusetts), 113, 129, 145
Hoar, Lewis Keith, 106
Hogarth, William, 146
Holyoke, Rev. Edward, 47
Hook, William, 89, 142
Howard, Thomas Sr., 111
Hubbard, Daniel, 61
Hughes, James, 139

I

Ince & Mayhew, 61
Ipswich (Massachusetts), 81

J

J E, 96
J P, 80
Japanned furniture, 80
Johnson, Alexander, 105
Johnson, Edmund, 64
Judson, Dr. Horace, 78
Judson, Grandpa, 78

K

Karolik Collection, 98, 99
Keeler, Hiram, 78
Keith, Francis, 106
Keith, Lewis, 106
King, Samuel, 125
King, William, 102
Kingston (Massachusetts), 6
Kingston (Rhode Island), 7
Kinsey, John P., 98

L

La Fondu, J....Jr., 138
Ladd House, 19
Langdon, J., 50
Latimer, Thomas, 40
Lee (Jeremiah) Mansion, 144
Lincoln, General Benjamin, 145
Lincoln, Zadoc, family, 75
Lisbon (Connecticut), 159
Litchfield (Connecticut), 78
Litchfield Historical Society, 96
Little, Arthur, 92
Little, Mrs. Nina Fletcher, 1, 102
Lockwood, Luke Vincent, 67
London Chair Makers' and Carvers book of Prices for Workmanship 1802, 89
Long, William, 38
Looking-glass makers: Cermenati & Bernada, 109
Looking glasses, 107-109
Loudon (New Hampshire), 102
Louisville (Kentucky), 139
Lovell, Mrs., 104

M

Macomber, W. A., 92
Macullas, Mrs. Mabel B., 130
Malden (Massachusetts), 129
Manwaring, Robert, 55
Marblehead (Massachusetts), 81
Martin, Ebenezer, 81
Marvin, James W., Collection, 82
Massachusetts furniture: beds, 1, 3, 6, 7; bookcase, 93; candlestands, 24, 26; chairs, 29-32, 36, 40, 43-45, 47-50, 53-56, 60-61, 63-67; chests, 71-72, 74-77, 80-81; clocks, 84; cupboards, 92-93; daybeds, 86-87; desks, 94, 95, 97-100, 106; dressing tables, 145; secretaries, 102, 104-105; sofas, 88-89; tables, 113, 129-136, 139, 142, 144, 145, 147; Windsor chairs, 156
Massachusetts Historical Society, 55
Massachusetts State House, 156
McKenzie, Kenneth, 63
Merrill, Gyles, 94
Merrill, J. Gyles, 94
Merrill, James C., 94
Merrill, Nathaniel, 94
Metropolitan Museum of Art, 29, 68, 69, 80, 83
Middletown (Connecticut), 17
Milton, 3
Minshall, 12
Mix, John, 58
Mix, Ruth (Stanley), 58
Moore, Cornelius C., Collection, 64, 111
Moore, David, 125
Morse, Moses, 102
Mount Holly (Vermont), 100
Mt. Vernon Place, Boston, 3
Museum of Fine Arts, Boston. *See* Collectors and Collections
Myers, L. G., 23, 26

N

New Britain (Connecticut), 58
New Brunswick, 83
New Castle (New Hampshire), 128
New Hampshire furniture: chairs, 43-44, 64; chests, 77; secretaries, 102, 103, 105; tables, 128
New Haven Colony Historical Society, 80
New Ipswich (New Hampshire), 77
New London County (Connecticut), 101
New Salem (Massachusetts), 100
Newbury (Massachusetts), 94
Newington (Connecticut), 34
Newport Historical Society, 52
Newport, Rhode Island, furniture: beds, 2, 3, 9, 11; chairs, 51, 52, 62, 68, 69; clock, 83; tables, 137, 140, 141
Nichols-Wanton-Hunter House, 3, 11
Norfolk (Virginia), 141
North Carolina, 56

North Shore, Massachusetts, furniture: chairs, 54; chests, 81; desks, 94
Norwich (Connecticut), 154
Noyes, Samuel, 77
Nutting Collection, Wadsworth Atheneum, 112

O

Old Deerfield, 98, 135
Old State House, Boston, 53
Old Sturbridge Village, 38, 50
Ostrander, 79
Owners (former) and donors: Allis, Mary, 72; Anonymous, 32, 71, 73, 76, 77, 97, 101, 106, 110, 116, 130, 159, 161, 162; Beal family, 113; Blair, Mrs. J. Insley, 8; Carr, Samuel, 9; Cooke, Helen Temple, 143; Damon, Harry E., 163; Dane family, 54, 55; Danforth, Margaret, 80; Fairbanks, Mrs. F. E., 100; Flayderman, Philip, 123, 138, 144; Fuessnich, Fred, 31; Garvan, Mrs. Francis P., 147; Grant, Moses, 100; Hadley, Francis C., 100; Halford, Mr. and Mrs. John, 1; Hanford, Mrs. Ernest J., estate of, 45, 57, 59, 75; Hoar, Lewis Keith, 106; Hoffmann, Henry A., 40, 127, 149, 150, 158; Hughes, James, 139; Hughes, Rose Anna (Fetter), 139; Judson, Dr. Horace, 78; Keith, Lewis, 106; Keith, Persis (Bigelow), 106; Lockwood, Luke Vincent, 67; Macullas, Mabel B., 130; Merrill, J. Gyles, 94; Merrill, James Cushing, 94; Merrill, Lucy (Cushing), 94; Mix family, 58; Myers, L. G., 23, 26, 47-49, 51, 60, 66, 69, 95, 99, 102, 119, 129, 134, 146, 148, 151, 154, 155; Palmer, Mrs. Austin, 118; Peck, Mr. and Mrs. Roger W., 96; Potter family, 7; Powell, Mrs. Grace E., 141; Saltonstall, Governor Gurdon, 143; Sampson, Mrs. Mary M., 29, 30; Schwartz, Walter·M. Jr., 152; Shaw, Francis G., 81; Sheperd, Eliza Y., 130; Shewmake, Lela, 117; Shute, Rev. Daniel, 129; Spelman, Henry Beale, 113; Stiles family, 82; Stribling, Dr. Francis Taliaferro, 141; Stribling, Henrietta Frances (Bragg Cuthbert), 141; Strong, Cotton, 100; Trefer-

then family, 128; Warner, Emily, 78; Warner, Reuben, 78; Wiederspohn, Mrs. J., 50; Wilcox, William family, 22; Wright, Deacon Samuel, 100; Wright, Sarah (Strong) Crowly, 100

P

Page, Blin W., 53
Paxton (Massachusetts), 106
Peck, Mr. and Mrs. Roger W., 96
Pembroke (Massachusetts), 129
Philadelphia, 61
Pickman family, 8, 55, 80
Pierce family, 47
Pimm, John, 80
Pinckney Street, 100
Poor, Enoch, 103
Portsmouth (New Hampshire), 47, 64
Potter family, 7
Providence (Rhode Island), 104, 111

Q

Quincy, Col. Josiah, 80

R

Rack, letter, 164
Rhode Island furniture: beds, 2, 3, 6, 9, 11, 19; candlestands, 22; chairs, 37, 48, 49, 51, 52, 57, 59, 62, 68, 69; clocks, 83; daybeds, 86, 87; desks, 99; sideboards, 111; tables, 120, 122, 125, 127, 137, 140, 141; Windsor chairs, 148-152, 154, 155, 157, 161
Rhode Island Historical Society, 111
Rhode Island School of Design, 104
Richmond (Virginia), 53
Robb, Mrs. Walter B., 6
Rockefeller, Abby Aldrich, Folk Art Collection, 58
Rueter, Mrs. Ernest, 98
Ruggles, Levi, 77
Rye (New Hampshire), 128

S

Salem (Massachusetts) furniture: chairs, 55, 56; sofas, 88, 89; tables, 131, 132, 142
Salem Towne House, 38
Salisbury (Massachusetts), 94
Saltonstall, Gurdon, 143
Sanders, Charles P., 79

Sanders family, 79
Sanders, John II, 79
Sanders, Maria (Elmendorf), 79
Sanders, Peter, 79
Savage, Mr. and Mrs. Norbert, 120
Saybrook (Connecticut), 36, 160
Schenectady (New York), 79
Scotia (New York), 79
Seaver, Joshua, 84
Secretaries, 101-105
Seymour family, 57
Seymour, George Dudley, Collection, 34
Seymour, John, 77, 104
Seymour, Thomas, 104
Shelburne Falls (Massachusetts), 100
Sheperd, Eliza Y., 130
Sheraton, Thomas, 88
Sherman, Mrs. Edward A., 125
Shute, Deborah (Cushing), 129
Shute, Mary (Cushing), 129
Shute, Rev. Daniel, 129
Sideboards, 110, 111
Skillin, John and Simeon, 3
Small, Edward, 71
Small, Jonathan, 71
Smith Collection, 145
Society for the Preservation of New England Antiquities, 139
Sofas, 88, 89
Southbury (Connecticut), 82
Stanley, Noah, 58
Stanley, Ruth, 58
Staunton (Virginia), 141
Stephenson, E., 53
Stone & Alexander, 100
Stone, Mr. and Mrs. Stanley, 131, 150
Storrs, Marmaduke, 83
Stribling, Dr. Francis Taliaferro, 141
Strong, Cotton, 100
Sudbury (Massachusetts), 77
Suffield (Connecticut), 45
Swan, H. S. Co., 100

T

Tables, 112, 114-127; breakfast, 130-132; bureau, 147; card, 140-142; corner, 134; dining, 136-139; dressing, 145, 146; drop-leaf, 133; folding, 113; gateleg, 135; marble top, 143, 144; side, 143, 144; tea, 128, 129
Talbot, Diana Wythe, 141
"Talbut," 57
Taunton (Massachusetts), 71

Numbers refer to catalog entries.

Taunton chests, 72
Ten Broeck, Albertina, 79
Ten Broeck, Jane Livingston, 79
Townsend, Job, 52, 87
Townsend, John, 83, 99
Tracy, Ebenezer, 159
Treferthen family, 128
Tuck, Samuel Jones, 156

V

Van Rensselaer-Crosby family, 93
Van Rensselaer, Elizabeth, 79
Virginia, 102, 105

W

Wadsworth Atheneum, 135
Wady, James, 83
Warner, Dr. Reuben, 78
Warren, Joseph, 102
Warren, Winslow family, 54
Westerly (Rhode Island), 22
Westmoreland County (Virginia), 40
Weymouth (Massachusetts), 129
Wilcox, William, family, 22
Willard, Aaron, 84
Willard, Aaron Jr., 85
Willard, Simon, 85
Windsor bench, 162

Windsor chairs, 148-161
Windsor (Connecticut), 112
Wingate, Love, 128
Winslow, Damaris, 71
Winterthur Museum. *See* Collectors
   and Collections
Wollaston (Massachusetts), 80
Woodbury (Connecticut), 82
Woodstock (Connecticut), 143
Wright, Deacon Samuel, 100
Wythe, George, 141

Z

Zutphen, W., 161

Numbers refer to catalog entries.

NEW ENGLAND FURNITURE AT WILLIAMSBURG

was composed in Baskerville (Fototronic) by Walter T. Armstrong, Inc., Philadelphia, Pennsylvania, and printed in photo-offset lithography by the Meriden Gravure Company, Meriden, Connecticut, on Mohawk Superfine paper. Color printing was done by W. M. Brown & Son, Richmond, Virginia, and binding by Haddon Craftsmen, Inc., Scranton, Pennsylvania. The book was designed by Richard J. Stinely.